Judge
For
Yourselves

Other books by Howard W. Boldt:
   The Gospel of the Rainbow Sign (2018) ISBN 9781773540665
   The Real Biblical Elder (2018) ISBN 9781773540672
   The Cure For Pentecostalism (2021) ISBN 9781773543635

Judge For Yourselves

Why head coverings for Christian worship and fellowship have always been optional

Howard W. Boldt

Copyright © 2021 Howard Boldt.
All rights reserved
No part of this publication may be reproduced, stored in a retrieval system, or transmitted in any form or by any means – electronic, mechanical, photocopy, recording or any other – except for brief quotations embodied in critical articles or printed reviews, without the prior written permission of the author.

ISBN: 978-1-77354-364-2

Published by Howard Boldt

Publishing Assistance and digital printing in Canada by

PageMaster.ca

Table of Contents

Preface v
Introduction vii
1   Church Delinquencies In Corinth 1
2   Head Covering in Scripture 7
3   Paul's Traditions 15
4   Head Covering & Hair Traditions 19
5   The Principles of Headship 27
6   The Woman's Rights 41
7   The Expected Admonition 47
8   Praying and Prophesying 53
9   The Actual Coverings 59
10   The Actual Grammar 65
11   The Infraction and The Offense 69
12   The Permission Imperative 77
13   Man's Obligation 81
14   Image and Glory 87
15   Fabric Or Authority 'Glory' 93
16   The Messengers 99
17   Judge Your Own Customs 103
18   'No Such Practice' 111
19   Worship Fashion 119
20   Judging Others 125

Preface

One of the great marvels of the gospel is its power to unite people from every ethnic background. Despite many different customs, true believers gather together to worship one God and fellowship with one another through Christ's sacrificial death and resurrection.

However, Christian fellowships are often divided by doctrines, that cannot be established in Scripture. Perhaps one of the most prominent examples of this is head covering etiquette for corporate worship. Most Christians believe that man's head was to be uncovered and woman's head covered, and applicable only to the apostolic churches. However, a significant minority believe that Paul never intended this custom to lapse. Worship head covering proponents, therefore, believe they are obeying Scripture. Alleged head covering regulation for worship is almost exclusively gleaned from Paul's letter to the Corinthians. (1 Cor.11) If the Scriptures are clear in all matters of faith and practice, then the Scriptures are sufficient to know God's will in this matter, too.

I had held the common view that a head covering was mandated as a custom for that time. The Lord commanded His disciples to wash one another's feet, and the Apostles exhorted believers to greet one another with a 'holy kiss'. As with the supposed head coverings mandate for women, I deemed these traditions optional.

Impetus for this analysis came from a friend who wanted an opinion on a book entitled Head Coverings by Jeremy Gardiner. Much of the reasoning in his book appears to be sound. However, for reasons in the chapters that follow, I could not agree with his conclusion that Paul required head covering for women in worship.

In this search for absolute answers on this important topic, it is my hope that the reader will also conclude, that the Scripture is abundantly clear on this matter.

Howard W. Boldt

Introduction

Paul's exhortation to the Corinthian church about head covering is still debated today. A minority of Christian churches today believe that the Apostle taught that women should cover their head during public worship. However, most teach that the alleged head covering traditions Paul required, were not part of a moral code and therefore, allows for changes according to different cultures in the world. (1 Cor. 11:1-16)

Commentaries presume various solutions to this dilemma. Most conservative commentators propose that head covering protocol was required for worship in the Apostolic era, but is no longer required today. But, if Paul had mandated a head covering custom, then why should it not be required today?

Before delving into Paul's exhortation, some artificial hurdles to accepting an apparently 'new' proper understanding of this portion of Scripture, must be challenged. I begin with 'translation issues'.

TRANSLATION ISSUES:

Inaccurate translation of Scripture may interfere with understanding a text correctly.

TRANSLATION DRIFT

Languages, into which the original Hebrew and Greek have been translated, change in time. Failing to translate contemporaneously, can contribute to the advancement of heresy. One such example is the word 'tongues'. In today's English we speak in languages not 'tongues' and it ought to be translated accordingly.[1]

DYNAMIC EQUIVALENCE

For the sake of greater clarity, translators insert words that are not in the original. This is known as 'dynamic equivalence.' Unless this principle is applied carefully, the translator may be editing the Scriptures rather than clarifying it. For example, 'gifts' has been inserted with 'spiritual' to make Paul say 'spiritual gifts'. This distorts the passage by making 'gifts' spiritual, when in reality, it's the <u>teachings</u> about all doctrine, including gifts, that are 'spirituals'. (1Cor.12:1 ;14:1) Another example is the

---

[1] Most popular translations such as the ESV, NASB, NKJV and NIV translate *glossa* as 'tongue'. (The New International Readers Version translates this as languages in 1 Cor. 14:5.)

insertion of the word 'office' or 'position'. Paul encourages the younger man who desires the 'work of oversight', not the office! (1 Tim.3:1) Relevant to the exposition in this book, the word 'symbol' is added in some translations, distorting the passage to read 'symbol of authority'. (1 Cor. 11:10)

TRANSLITERATION

The Greek for 'angel' has been transliterated, rather than translated. It should always be 'messenger' – always. It should be left to the reader to determine if the messenger is a man or a heavenly being.

INTERPRETATION PRINCIPLES

Yet, even when the translations are adequate, passages are erroneously interpreted. Almost unanimous in the belief that Paul did exhort believers to comply with one head covering custom, commentators have initiated a dilemma that did not exist during Apostolic era and before. While it is good to check other Bible commentaries, scholars, and ministers, the believer's final authority isn't the professional. The Bereans didn't say, 'We should check with our 'pastor'.' The Bereans examined OT Scripture for themselves; we should too.

The New Testament (NT) did not replace the Old Testament (OT). The New Testament record of Christ's work, is verified by the prophecies of His work in the Old Testament. When Jesus taught Nicodemus the new birth, He was teaching him vital OT truth from Psalms 87.

In most cases, allegorical and literal figures of speech, are easily discerned. For example, when John the Baptist said, 'Behold the Lamb of God'..., we know that 'Lamb' symbolizes Christ.

Broader cultural context gleaned from extra-biblical sources must be current to the apostolic era. It should not be assumed that traditions practiced since Bible times, proves Bible customs. For example, it is impossible to determine the correct mode of baptism from post-apostolic history. Similarly, head covering practices since the apostolic church do not prove a biblical regulation or practice.

Again, the Bereans compared Paul's teachings with OT scriptures to verify what they heard. If indeed, head covering was required, especially for worship, it would be expected that the OT would provide some evidence and reasons for it. A sound understanding of the NT is compromised, if the OT is ignored.

INTERPRETING BASED ON EXPIRED CUSTOMS

To accommodate the notion that head covering is no longer a mandated custom, some have argued, myself included, that as Christ's command to wash one another's feet and Paul's command to greet one another with a holy kiss are not universally applicable, neither is head coverings. (Jn.13:14; 1 Cor. 16:19) Others argue that the <u>supposed</u> head covering imperative has not expired because it symbolizes man and woman's relation to one another under God. But, why then, should we not continue with the ancient custom of 'foot washing' as a means of showing others how Christ humbled Himself to serve us? It is incongruous to argue that the 'holy kiss' and 'foot washing' are no longer required, while a head covering custom is. If a tradition, such as head covering, is part of a moral code, then it must be explained why other meaningful traditions like foot-washing and the 'holy kiss' are no longer practiced, at least in western churches.

'NATURAL' READING VERSUS 'ACTUAL' READING

The notion, among some that a 'new' biblical interpretation cannot contradict a 'normal' or 'natural' reading of the passage, is presumptuous.

A prominent example of how a 'normal' reading of a text can get one into serious theological problems is the doctrine of works. Professing believers still get the doctrine of salvation wrong. Misunderstanding James' teaching of faith and works, theologians continue to default to the 'natural' reading of the text, that one is saved by means of both faith and works. (Jas. 2:14, 24) Upon careful examination, the 'natural' reading of the text is not the <u>actual</u> meaning of the text. James was describing the character of faith. He said that the result of true faith in God is works. Saving faith is accompanied by works. This accords with Paul, who writes that no man can contribute to his salvation by his works. (Eph. 2:8,9)

Baptism is another doctrine where professing Christians are distracted with the 'normal' or natural reading of a text. Most of Christianity so-called, believe baptism is necessary for salvation. When Paul preached the gospel to the Philippian jailor, the normal reading of the passage seems to indicate the necessity of baptism for salvation. (Ac. 16:31) But when compared with other Scripture, it becomes clear that Paul could not have intended baptism as a step to conversion. The thief on the cross went to Paradise without being baptized. The actual reading of any text about conversion, does not require baptism.

Even Christ's disciples had not understood that His kingdom would not obliterate the Roman empire. The disciples needed the 'new' interpretation, which was that Christ came to die for a kingdom that was not of this world. They, like us, read naturally, or hear presumptively.

SUMMARY

Credible interpretation is not based on assumptions or bias. Translation, grammar, immediate context and culture help to determine if one's 'natural' reading of many puzzling scriptural passages, is also the 'actual' reading. Head coverings in 1 Cor. 11 is one of those Scriptures.

THE CHURCH FATHERS

Defenders of a worship head covering custom appeal to the 'Church Fathers', who promoted the practice. Because they lived closer to the times of the Apostles, scholars surmise that they knew the expected custom. But is this reasoning valid? And, are they trustworthy?

THEIR THEOLOGY IS AMBIGUOUS

The "theology of the fathers is much less than ideal, since it does not recognize the Pauline writings on par with the Old Testament scriptures, and at times, it seems to have an inadequate emphasis on grace."[2]

The doctrine of eternal security, better known as 'the perseverance of the saints', was not carefully delineated by the early church Fathers. In fact, NT references vital to this doctrine were scarce in over 5000 pages of Ante-Nicene writings. (100 AD to Council of Nicaea in 325 AD) For example, John 3:16 is referenced twice; Rom.8:33,34, once; John 6:37,39, four times; Jn.10:28,29, twice; Eph.1:13-14, seven; Phil.1:6, zero; 1 Pet.1:4,5, zero. Though eternal security is not explicitly denied, it is argued that when all the extracts of pertinent scripture are surveyed, the 'fathers' had no clear understanding of what they were trying to teach, consequently, falling into contradictions.[3]

THEIR PRACTICES WERE CONTRIVED

After the Apostles, Christendom drifted into various doctrinal fallacies. Church Fathers, like Tertullian, is cited as a support for the practice of head covering.[4] He held to mortification of the body such as

---

[2] Dr. Peter A. Lillback, Testamentum Imperium, An International Theological Journal , p.3
http://www.preciousheart.net/ti/2007/005_07_Lillback_Early_Saints.pdf

[3] ibid. p.14

[4] Jeremy Gardiner, *Head Coverings*, p.10

fasting, wearing sackcloth and ashes, for sins committed after baptism. Irenaeus, Origen, Tertullian and Ambrose taught that baptism is necessary for salvation.[5] Tertullian, Chrysostom and Augustine believed in a purging of the believer after death. Clement contributed to the doctrine of purgatory and mysticism.[6]

THEIR DOCTRINES CONFLICT WITH SCRIPTURE
Church Fathers held to some very erroneous views.

> "Clement and Tertullian had ascribed eternal virginity to Mary. Augustine believed that the mother of the sinless Christ had never committed actual sin. Monasticism, with its emphasis upon virginity, strengthened the idea of the virginity of Mary."[7]

Clement contributed to the false doctrines of purgatory and mysticism.[8] Tertullian became ensnared in Montanism, which claimed a 'new era of prophecy and continuing revelation.'[9] Irenaeus, Origen, Tertullian and Ambrose taught that baptism is necessary for salvation.[10]

Revered among the 'fathers' is Augustine who lived three centuries after the apostles. At first, he held that the miraculous gifts of the Spirit had ceased, but later changed his view.

> "But there is still a major problem with Augustine's report of miracles. His description is highly mystical and replete with superstitious elements. In recording these healings, he attributes them to things like prayer to the saints, the power of relics, and the use of religious symbols. Such descriptions are deeply troubling and call into serious question the veracity of his supposed miracles. Added to that, most of what he reports is from second or third-hand sources, which again casts doubt on the factual accuracy of his interpretations."[11]

---

[5] Christian Apologetics and Research Ministry
https://carm.org/church-fathers-quotes-topic

[6] Howard F. Vos, *Exploring Church History*, Thomas Nelson Publishers, 1994, p.19

[7] Earle Cairns, *Christianity Through the Centuries*, 1964 P. 174

[8] Howard F. Vos, *Exploring Church History*, Thomas Nelson Publishers, 1994, p.19

[9] Ibid., P. 18, 32

[10] Christian Apologetics and Research Ministry
https://carm.org/church-fathers-quotes-topic

[11] Nathan Busenitz, *Augustine and Miracles in History*, Point #7. The Cripplegate
https://thecripplegate.com/augustine-and-miracles-in-history/

Augustine's understanding of faith, grace and practice are fundamentally conflicted.

CONCLUSION

Church Fathers certainly give the modern student insight to the traditions and beliefs of their day, but not their accuracy. Paul predicted that after His departure salvage wolves would come. (Acts 20:29-31) Along with Judaism, most of Christendom after the Apostles drifted into the false doctrine of salvation by works. The supposed eminence of Church Fathers is just that – supposed. Believers must be wary of Church Fathers.

The credibility of Church Fathers is not enhanced, despite having lived closer to the time of the Apostles. Neither were they in agreement with one another. The Church Fathers were the predecessors to Roman Catholicism.

While some Church Fathers may be fundamentally correct on doctrines such as the depravity of man and the substitutionary death of Christ, there are other essential doctrines. Clearly, Augustine and other church Fathers promoted doctrines that interfere with the salvation of the lost and the growth of believers. Having failed this test of orthodoxy, they are also suspect for anything they have written about the custom of head coverings in the church.

Church Fathers Contribute Nothing To The Head Covering Practice

Biblical head covering customs cannot be extrapolated from those practiced in the second century and onward. The majority view in church history does not determine truth; the Scripture does. The 'Church Fathers' do not confirm Scripture. Scripture certifies Scripture. If an ancient writer cannot get some of the basics right pertaining to the salvation of the lost and the sanctification of the believer, why should we trust his commentary of 1 Corinthians 11?

SCHOLARSHIP

Negative commentary expressed in this book on biblical scholarship requires a proviso. It is important to highlight the importance of scholarship. While scholars have taught error, they have also been greatly used of God in the defense of the faith of our Lord. In this book, I have used degreed individuals who know Hebrew, Greek and are experts in disciplines that I am not. I appreciate them. And I need them to help me understand various portions of scripture, especially in regards to grammar and history. However, noted, reputable, conservative scholars differ on a variety of biblical doctrine. Opposing views is evidence that not all scholars are right. Therefore, the reader should hold every commentator, including this author, accountable to the Scriptures, not to other commentators. All views, 'new' and 'old', are subject to the Scriptures.

SCHOLARSHIP CAN MISLEAD

Scholars are intelligent. But intelligence is not enough. Satan is also very smart. Knowing what God had said to Adam, he was able to twist his words to deceive Eve. Scholars believe in evolution. They also believe in the apparently 'new' teachings of psychology and self-esteem, which are just a rehash of Satan's temptation to Eve in Eden, that she could become as gods. Therefore, it is important to know the boundaries of error, beyond which Bible scholars become false teachers.

I think the conservative Christian would agree that there are some doctrines that do not interfere with the salvation of the lost and the growth of the believer. Whether one's eschatology is ammillennial or dispensational, though important, such differences do not contribute to a false gospel of eternal salvation. However, when reputable reformed theologians teach salvation by faith alone insist, as some have, that head covering is necessary for worship, they have introduced doctrine that affects a believer's walk with God. What did the Lord really say? Are head coverings required to grow in Christ?

NOVELTY

To the extent that publishers have ministered the gospel pertaining to salvation and sanctification, true believers should be grateful.

CORRECT 'NEW' VIEWS HAVE NOT BEEN PUBLISHED

Having gained notoriety by nailing the 95 theses to the castle door in Wittenberg, Luther printers wanted to print his books. His works were a hot commodity. From the time of Luther, printing houses published marketable material. Contemporary publishers, likewise, look for reputation and potential for sales. Is the 'author' well-known? The 'praise' pages evidence the author's need to gain academic credibility with the endorsement of other well-educated published professionals.

Luther's publication of 'new' doctrines on the Lord's Table, known as consubstantiation, was wrong. On the other hand, his published views against indulgences, penance, etc., were considered 'new' by many in his day. His correct published views on the "bondage of the will' was also 'new' at the time. Therefore, sound doctrine cannot be based on a perception of age.

Believers in every age have failed to correctly discern 'old' truth. Consequently, 'new' false doctrines emerge when 'old' true doctrines are forgotten. Then, when 'old' doctrine is rediscovered decades or centuries later, they are 'new'. Therefore, any 'new' previously unpublished observations, passing the test of biblical veracity, including those presented in this book, were certainly known by believers centuries earlier. Rediscovered previously unknown biblical truth is personally 'new', not historically 'new'.

Very 'old' truth had been known in Israel. But as they drifted from the Lord, His word became unknown. King Josiah was alarmed when he heard the newly discovered Book of the Law read to him. (2 Kg. 22:8-13) To him, the scripture was 'new', but it had been given long ago.

OLD' TRUTH MIGHT BE 'NEW'

To the extent that publishers have ministered the gospel pertaining to salvation and sanctification, true believers should be grateful. Yet, Christian publishers have, in some measure, failed to correctly discern 'old' biblical truth. Then when generally unknown 'old' biblical truth becomes known, it is 'new'. Biblical truth is 'new' when 'old' truth is rediscovered.

The 'New' Truth That Nicodemus Should Have Known

After explaining to Nicodemus, a teacher in Israel, that one must be born again to enter the kingdom of God, He asks him, 'Are you a teacher in Israel, yet do not know these things?' Jesus implied that the doctrine of the new birth is taught in the OT. (Psa. 87) This teaching was 'new' to Nicodemus, but not new to Scriptures. It was and is still 'old' truth!

The 'New' Truth That The Disciples Should Have Known

At the Last Supper Jesus gave His disciples a 'new' commandment to follow. (Jn.13:34) They argued with one another who would be the greatest in the kingdom of heaven. Washing one another's feet was the last thing on their mind. (Lk.22:24). But long ago, Moses had commanded the people to love their neighbor as themselves, so it was not new. (Lev. 19:18,34) However, by their behavior, the disciples demonstrated that this commandment was new to them, not new in existence.

The Source Of 'New' And 'Old' Truth

Every 'teaching' ought to be tested according to the 'old' truth of the Scriptures, not when it was discovered. Therefore, to say that a 'new view cannot be true', is false.

A 'New' View Might Be False

Peter warned believers that false prophets would arise to introduce heresies about the Lord. (2 Pe. 2:1-2) Paul was amazed at how quickly the Galatian churches had succumbed to a 'different' gospel. (Ga. 1:6,7) Believers were to reject 'new' views that twisted the gospel of the Lord Jesus Christ.

An 'Old' View Might Be False

For centuries it was believed that the sun revolved around the earth. Even as early as the third century BC, Aristarchus of Samoa proposed that the earth actually revolved around the sun. Evidently, it was not until the 16th century that Copernicus challenged the geocentric model and it became known that indeed the earth revolved around the sun. [12] Interestingly, when heliocentrism was first made known, it was not well received by the 'Church' because it was 'new'. Yet, what was 'old' and believed to be true, was false.

Summary

Gaging the veracity of apparently 'new' teaching, such as found in this book, based on opinions of what is 'old' or 'new', does not determine truth. If a teaching is deemed to be 'new', it is either because it is contrived or because it is rediscovered. 'Old' does not make doctrine right any more than 'new' makes doctrine wrong. A 'new' teaching might be 'new' because 'old' truth had been unknown. All views, both right and wrong, have at one time been 'new'. Whether 'old' or 'new', therefore, it is vital to know whether the teaching is 'new' to the Scriptures.

Therefore, in the quest for the truth of the Scriptures, adages such as 'what's new is probably not true' or 'what's older is probably true', are of absolutely no value. These are not biblical principles.

---

[12] McKay, Hill, Buckler, *A History Of Western Society*, Sixth Edition, Houghton Mifflin Company, P. 96,126

Conclusion

The teaching of this book may be new to Christians, but is it new to Scripture? If these apparently 'new' teachings of this book harmonize with the Bible, it is absolutely certain that this author has not been the first to teach it. Believers, acquainted with the Bible through the centuries, would have known and expressed exactly what Paul had been teaching on head covering. Obscured by faulty translations, presumptive interpretation, and Church Fathers, some correct views remained unpublished and thus became isolated and generally unknown. A view not found in centuries of published Christian literature, does not make it unacceptable.

It is therefore important to highlight the fact that sound biblical scholarship is not dependent on published opinions. It is dependent on the illumination of the Holy Spirit, who is not restricted to Bible colleges and seminaries. Ultimately, the Bible is the only published 'view' that matters, because it's the truth without error.

The 'Majority' Argument For Orthodoxy

Church history is replete with the practice of head covering. Believing the majority practiced the tradition of head covering, people assume this practice to be biblical. How do the 'majority' fare in Scripture? The majority of 'Christians' are on the broad way that leads to destruction. The narrow way never was a majority view, even in matters pertaining the essentials of the faith. (Matt. 7:13,14; 20:16) The majority of 'Christians' today believe that Peter was the first Pope, based on an erroneous interpretation of Matt. 16:17-19. The majority believe that baptism is required for membership in Christ's church.

Most of Christianity today is a laboratory that continues to infect people with these old contrived doctrinal viruses. Evangelical churches of twenty or thirty years ago have vanished.

A Basis For Critical Analysis

A critique of this book is not based on what centuries of ecclesial authorities have taught. However, the basis of a biblical critical analysis of this or any other book about the Bible must pertain to its two central themes – the salvation of the lost and the sanctification of the believer.

Does a wrong view of the head covering custom teach professing Christians a salvation by works? Or, does a wrong view of the head covering custom impede the spiritual growth of a believer? Only the Bible has the final answer.

Literal Translation

1 Corinthians 11:1-16

1) Be imitators of me in works, speech and attitude, as I am of Christ.

2) Moreover, I commend you that in all things you have remembered me even as I delivered to you the teachings (traditions) you are keeping.

3) Moreover, I desire you to know that Christ is the head of every man. Moreover, the head of the woman is the man, of Christ - God.

4) Every man praying or prophesying with anything down from his head, he dishonors the head of him.

5) Moreover, every woman praying or prophesying with her head uncovered dishonors the head of her; one indeed she is with one who is shaven.

6) Indeed, if a woman does not cover her head, permit her also to sheer herself. Moreover, if it is shameful to a woman to be shorn or to be shaven, permit her to cover her head.

7) Accordingly (given the practice of this custom, truly), it is reasoned then that man is not indebted to cover the head, being the image and glory of God, but the woman is the glory of man. ['indebted' is in the present indicative, not imperative]

8) And indeed, the man is not of woman, but woman of man.

9) Truly, indeed man was not created on account of the woman but woman on account of the man.

10) For this reason [on account of this] the woman is due authority to have on the head, through [by means of, via] the messengers.

11) However, neither is woman separate from man or man separate from woman, in the Lord.

12) Indeed, just as the woman is of the man, so also the man by the woman is; moreover all things are of God.

13) In you yourselves judge: fitting is it for a woman to be unveiled to God to pray?

14) Does not even comparing nature itself teach that indeed if a man have long hair a dishonor to him it is?

15) A woman however, if she have long hair, it is glory to her; for the long hair instead, as a covering [mantle] is given to her.

16) Moreover, if anyone is inclined to be contentious, we have no such practice nor the churches of God.'

The above translation is based on Bible Hub Interlinear Bible.
https://biblehub.com/interlinear/1_corinthians/11.htm

It is advised that all translations, including the one above, be evaluated and compared to the Greek.

Abbreviations

OT is Old Testament; NT is New Testament; YLT is Young's Literal Translation. NAS is New American Standard. KJV is King James Version; NKJV is New King James Version. ESV is English Standard Version.

1 Church Delinquencies In Corinth

The Corinthian church had numerous conflicts. Paul's exhortations for correction and his approach to discipline of believers, provide context necessary to avoid contradictory inferences from his counsel on head covering. Even a brief summary of the conditions prevalent in the Corinthian church, will provide a strong indication of whether head covering regulations harmonized or clashed with Paul's teaching, and identify those who thought the head covering tradition was important.

Through Paul's gospel ministry in Corinth, many believed and were baptized. (Acts 18:8) Paul expressed gratitude that they were enriched in Christ through the spoken word with all necessary knowledge for a blameless appearing before the Lord. (1 Cor. 1:4-7)

BEHAVIOR OF THE CHURCH

Paul left Corinth, with Aquila and Priscilla, to serve in Ephesus. Men from Corinth informed him about the church. All was not well. So, he sent them a letter that exposed what should have been an embarrassing review of their attitude and behavior. At the beginning of his letter, Paul hints at superiority complex issues. (1:10,11) Some were manipulated to think that their abilities were inferior to others. (12:21,22) Some thought themselves deficient in giftedness, thus lacking a confirmation of their testimony. (1:6,7; 12:23) Others boasted in worldly wisdom, rather than the Lord. (2:6)

THEIR GATHERINGS WERE DISORDERLY

It is supposed that the Corinthian church was a hub of supernatural miracles, healings, the speaking of unlearned languages with new revelations from God.[13] Nothing in Paul's letter supports this notion.

Those who were not conversant in the Greek vernacular, likely understood it. But, some, who were speaking other learned languages, could not be understood. Inappropriate use of native languages in

---

[13] Howard W. Boldt, *The Cure For Pentecostalism*, P. 149, The author deals with the context and grammar of 1 Cor. 12-14 to show that the Corinthians did not speak miraculous in foreign languages, or gibberish. God is not the author of confusion.

assembly was just one example of Corinthian immaturity. Both men and women were competing for opportunity to be heard in their meetings, so much so, that a visitor would have considered them crazy. (14:18-20)

THEY TOOK THEIR GRIEVANCES TO SECULAR COURTS

Among them were professing believers who took one another to the secular law courts. The wisdom craze had affected their thinking on law. They wondered how the church could provide fair judgment when the 'wisdom' established in Greek jurisprudence was centuries old? Yet, Paul asks them if there is a wise man among them. (6:1-8) The just and moral principles of His word predate anything the Greeks could offer. As professing believers, they had greater confidence in the secular courts.

THEY OFFENDED THE CONSCIENCES OF OTHERS

Paul had instructed this church how not to offend in matters that, under normal circumstances, were not wrong. Though believers could eat meat sacrificed to idols without causing personal spiritual harm, the consciences of new converts from pagan religions were offended by it. (1 Cor. 8:1-13; 10:23-33) They were oblivious to the spiritual growth of new believers and how they might jeopardize their witness to unbelievers.

THEY HAD BECOME SECTARIAN

Sectarianism was already flourishing in this church. Fellowship in the church had become divided.

Partisanship Was Based on Leader Preference

Paul had admonished these believers and professing believers for their favoritism of one leader over another. Whether Christ, Paul, Cephas or Apollos, their theology was the same, so this was no reason to be partisan. Some distinguished themselves by who baptized them. Motivated by envy and strife, they divided on issues having nothing to do with essential doctrine. (1:10-13; 3:3) They had become political.

Partisanship Was Based on Possessions

They despised others by ignoring their needs. Some at the Lord's Table belonged to the Selfish Party. (11:17-22) Those having sufficient food were not concerned for some among them who were hungry.

Partisanship Based on Status

Slaves were to be considered brothers in Christ. (7:21-24; 12:13) Having been purchased by the blood of Christ they enjoyed the same spiritual status as every other believer.

Partisanship Was Based on Ethnicity

Jews and Gentiles were offending one another, oblivious to the fact that, as believers, they were part of one body. (10:32: 12:13)

Partisanship Was Based In Tradition

Paul reminded the Jews that religious traditions, such as circumcision, were of no avail. (7:18, 19)

Partisanship Was Based on Gifts

Some were excluded because of their apparent lack of ability, being weak, impotent and without strength. The 'less honorable' were excluded by embarrassment. (12:22-25)

WORLDLY INFLUENCES IN THE CHURCH

Ethnic constituents of the church were impacted negatively by so-called wisdom and signs. Jews and Gentiles were influenced by culture.

WISDOM

Worldly philosophies in the church elicited a quest for wisdom contrary to Christ. (1:20-31) So, Paul addressed their special regard for 'intellectual' abilities with a quote from Isaiah that God will destroy the wisdom of the wise. (Isa.29:14) Human acumen cannot make the gospel appear intellectual and wise. (1:18-21) Consequently, the Gentiles mostly rejected the gospel as foolish.

SIGNS

Paul noted the Jewish obsession with signs. (1:22; Acts 18:1-12) The Jews would not accept the sign unless it aligned with their own contrived theology, so Christ remained a stumbling block to them. Jesus spoke of the sign-seeking Jews as an evil generation. (Mt.16:4; Lk.11:29-32)

IGNORANCE OF SCRIPTURE

As is evident from their conduct, even essential doctrines had been obscured and ignored. They were 'doctrinally challenged'.

FALSE DOCTRINE OF INCLUSIVISM

Paul thanks God that the testimony of Christ had been confirmed in them, but he is under no illusion that all who heard his letter read, were converted. He writes specifically to "those who are called to be saints". (1Cor. 1:2-8) Uncertain of a professing believer's conversion, Paul counsels the others not to associate with this so-called brother in order that he might repent. (5:11) He provides evidence of belligerence that would prevent some from entry into the kingdom. (6:9,10) Paul is concerned for some among them who did not have a credible profession of faith. He speaks to them as infants in Christ, as a people whose spiritual growth had been stunted, wondering if some among them were even converted. They were still walking as mere men, that is, the natural man. Were they of the Spirit or of the flesh? (3:1-3) Some had not examined themselves to see if they were of the faith at the Lord's Table. Paul also warned the church about the possibility of believing in vain. (11:28,29; 15:2) In another letter, he again exhorts professing believers to examine themselves to see if they were of the faith. (2 Cor. 13:5)

FALSE DOCTRINE OF 'GIFTED' REVELATION

Contrary to much of what is taught, the Corinthians were unaware that they were not the source of truth. (2:10-16) They were not 'gifted' to reveal new truth. Rather, Paul exhorted them to be interested in 'spirituals', which means 'teachings', not gifts. (12:1; 14:10) He does not compliment them for exercising their gifts. Yet, because expositors and translators have introduced confusion into Paul's clear teaching on 'spirituals', we have fallen for the mistaken notion that the Corinthian church was a center for new revelation. (translators erroneously replace the noun 'spirituals' with 'gifts')

Notwithstanding the false teaching of the Charismatics and Continuationists, the Cessationists also teach that the Corinthians were 'gifted' by the Holy Spirit to speak forth truth not previously revealed.[14] (13:8) One Cessationist concludes:

> "Therefore the gift of prophecy can be defined as the supernatural ability to receive revelation from God and to communicate it to others in the people's language."[15]

Another Cessationist opines on the gift of prophecy,

> "The "revelation" is such as was given to prophets [14:30]. It was the Holy Spirit's unveiling of a mystery and incorporates an

---

[14] Cessationists believe that 'languages shall cease' refers to a gift of speaking languages believers had not learned, but ended in the apostolic era (1Cor. 13:8) The problem with that argument is that we still speak languages today. However, it is true that the languages spoken in Corinth have ceased. Today's Greek is not the same as the Corinthian Greek.

[15] Larry D. Pettegrew, *The New Covenant Ministry of the Holy Spirit*, Kress Biblical Resources, 2001, p.163

implementation of the word of wisdom [1 Cor.2:6-7; 12:8; 13:2]. The gift involved immediate inspiration of a prophet."[16] (emphasis added)

To prophesy is simply the ability to understand and communicate knowledge, whether it comes from God or another person. As God revealed his will to Moses his prophet, Moses in turn would reveal God's will to Aaron, Moses' prophet. (Ex. 7:1) Unlike Aaron, however, the Corinthians gave no evidence that they correctly taught scripture, in fact, they exceeded it. (1 Cor. 4:6,7) Every believer's access to the gift of 'prophecy' involves the transmission of already revealed truth by the illumination of the Holy Spirit.

If The Corinthian Prophets Were Revelatory, Why Did Paul Write?
Therefore, the belief that these Corinthians were actually speaking in languages they had not learned, and prophesying truth not yet revealed is contrary to the text and context of this Scripture.[17] Had these believers truly been revealing new truth as alleged by 'cessationists' and 'continuationists', why did Paul have to write them this letter? Why had the Corinthians not already been prophesying the much-needed truth Paul had revealed to them? Had these Corinthian 'prophets' been revealing new truth, why did Paul have to write them about their deficiencies? Why did the Holy Spirit not reveal to the Corinthian 'prophets' what He had revealed to Paul? The fact is that God never did speak to these Corinthians by revelation except by the OT writings and the Apostles. They had the same OT Scriptures the Bereans had. They had all the truth they needed, but failed to demonstrate the Berean gift of prophecy. The fact is that no one in Corinth spoke a language they had not learned and no one in Corinth prophesied truth that had not already been revealed in the Scriptures.

SUMMARY

The behavioral and doctrinal delinquencies of the Corinthian church unveiled in Paul's letter, indicate major deficiencies in their understanding of salvation and sanctification. They were oblivious to the fornication of a man living with his father's wife. (5:1,12) They ignored those who were hungry at the Lord's Table, they were disorderly in the

---

[16] Robert L. Thomas, *Understanding Spiritual Gifts*, Kregel Publications, 1999, p.108

[17] Howard Boldt, *The Cure For Pentecostalism*, chapters. 8,11,12

services and didn't know things they should have known. They competed with one another in minor issues through the secular courts. (6:1-8) They quarreled about leadership. They were sectarian. Would we be thrilled with a letter from the Apostle Paul, such as he wrote to the Corinthians, read aloud to the congregations of our churches? These Corinthians, for the most part, lacked spiritual discernment for all matters pertaining to faith and practice.

They had exceeded what was written. (4:6-10; 14:37) Throughout his letter to the Corinthians he asks them, 'do you not know?' Note how very forceful Paul's words are in dealing with self-sufficiency. He even asks if he should come with a rod? (4:8-13,18-21)

What About Head Covering?

Apparently negligent in various essential matters pertaining to salvation and sanctification, head covering worship protocol became another distraction from the gospel. Could there be any among them who could discern matters of spiritual importance? And what would we expect them to know about the OT scriptures? Is there any evidence that they approached this matter as the Bereans did?

It is unreasonable to expect that this church would have the discernment necessary for God-honoring worship and fellowship.

2 Head Covering in Scripture

Since Paul's exhortation pertains to headwear while praying and prophesying, it is important to know if etiquette protocols had already been established in Scripture. (11:4, 5) Was God ever displeased with men praying and prophesying with their heads covered or with woman's head uncovered? Before examining Paul's text on head covering, it is helpful to be acquainted with the OT passages he knew on this topic.

If we were to find support from this Apostle for a head covering tradition, we would certainly expect him to argue for it from the Scriptures, as he did on other matters. If head coverings in corporate worship were not regulated in the OT, then inferences from 1 Corinthians chapter 11 that they were, are problematic.

OT INCIDENTS OF HEAD COVERING

Paul quoted from the OT in 1 Corinthians 17 times, and alludes to it over 20 times.[18] Had Paul been exhorting believers for failing to observe a previously commanded custom for corporate worship? Had God defined headwear worship custom in the OT, 'dishonoring' one's head might then be sin. Following is a list of OT head covering occurrences:

- Seeing Isaac, Rebekah covered herself with a veil. (Gen. 24:65)
- Moses prophesied with his head covered. (Ex. 34:32-35)
- Moses forbade Aaron and his sons Eleazar and Ithamar, to uncover their heads in grief, when God struck Nadab and Abihu for offering strange fire before the Lord. (Lev. 10:6)
- When charged with adultery before the priest, the woman's hair was to be uncovered. (Num. 5:18) Some say 'uncover' means to loosen the hair, others say that it means to remove head covering.
- Judah mistakenly judged a veiled woman to be a harlot. (Gen. 38:14,15)
- The High Priest wore a miter and the other priests wore caps. (Ex. 28:4,37,40; 29:6,9)

---

[18] Blue Letter Bible
https://www.blueletterbible.org/study/misc/quotes03.cfm

- David and his men covered their heads in grief. (2 Sam. 15:30)
- Heads were covered, embarrassed for having failed to get water. (Jer. 14:3,4)
- Haman covered his head in grief because he was assigned to honor Mordecai. (Est. 6:12)
- David prayed publicly with his head covered! (2 Sam.15:30-32)
- Apparently, Hannah did not wear a veil when praying in public, because Eli was able to see her lips moving. (1 Sam. 1:12,13)
- Boaz filled Ruth's veil with grain, which implies that she was then not covered. (Ruth 3:15)
- The Shulamite woman wore a head covering. (Song of S. 5:7)
- Ezekiel prophesied with his head covered. (Ez. 24:15-21)

Both Moses and Ezekiel prophesied with their heads covered. In the temple service of God, the priests wore head covering. In the presence of the people David prayed with his head covered. Furthermore, these examples indicate that women did not feel shame, when they were not wearing a veil or head covering in public.

Except for the priests and servers in the Temple, no universal head-covering imperatives were issued to men or women for worship in the OT. Had there been a ruling that converted priests not cover their heads while praying and prophesying, the Apostles and elders would have said so, as they had done with circumcision. (Acts 6:7) There is no teaching in the OT that mandates or even hints that the general public must observe a head covering tradition for worship.

God's View of Outward Appearance

Both Testaments teach principles that show God's approach to physical appearance.

How Did Samuel, The Prophet Choose a King?

Samuel, the Prophet, was told not to judge a man by his outward appearance in his search for a king; God looks on the heart. (1 Sa.16:7) God does not delight in the strength of the horse, or man, but in those who fear Him. (Psa. 147:10,11) God is impressed with neither human power or appearance.

How Did Jesus Teach His Disciples to Pray?

Had Christ been offended by a violation of head covering custom, we should find evidence of this in His interaction with the disciples when He taught them to pray. But nothing is said regarding head covering. Given the lack of any uniformity of custom regarding head covering, there is no reason to infer that man would know that communal prayer should always occur with head uncovered.

WHAT DID JESUS THINK ABOUT THE PHARISEES' APPEARANCE?

The Pharisees misinterpreted Scripture and devised phylacteries to be mounted on the left arm and on the forehead. (Matt. 23:5) They walked around unkempt to impress others that they had fasted. They cleaned the outside of the cup. (Lk. 11:39) Jesus called them hypocrites.

Speaking to these experts of outward appearance, Jesus said, "Even so you also outwardly appear righteous to men, but inside you are full of hypocrisy and lawlessness." (Matt.23:28, NKJV) Now, instead of seeing a dressed-up Pharisee as an upstanding clergyman, the people would wonder about what Jesus knew and they didn't.

SUMMARY

Certainly, Christ had nothing against those who dressed well. But He admonished any who depended on outward appearance to commend themselves to God. What would Christ say about head coverings?

Looking Spiritual

The Pharisees and the scribes were adept at looking 'heavenly'. With their phylacteries, enlarged borders on their garments, they distinguished themselves from the people. Jesus described them as beautiful on the outside but full of dead men's bones. (Matt.23:5, 27) As will become evident, this head covering issue was another attempt by the 'spiritual' religious to impose their view of what men and women should look like on the outside, during prayer and prophesying. (11:4,5) This is a perfect opportunity for the devil and the flesh to make Christians and professing Christians feel good, by portraying godliness they don't have.

Does God Hear Prayer Based on Appearance?

Are we to believe that when men prayed with their heads covered as some Jews did, that God was disgraced and that He would not hear them? Did God express disappointment in any woman who prayed with her head uncovered or that she might be dishonoring man as her head? Nowhere in scripture are His people told that they must comply with heavenly head covering protocol for God to accept our worship. God hears our prayers based upon our heart, not according to an outward custom.

Indeed, some customs are an honorable way of expressing the attitude of the heart. Dressing in sackcloth ashes was a means of expressing sorrow for sin before a just and holy God. Yet, all expressions of contriteness, were personally initiated, not legislated. It seems that if there was any kind of dress suitable for some in the Corinthian church, this would have been it. How would head covering rules have been any different than the Pharisaical approach to spirituality?

ALLEGED PURPOSE FOR CUSTOM

It is alleged that Paul invokes the head covering custom for the purpose of distinguishing creation order and roles. (11:7-10) If that were so, then why was this tradition not mandated in the OT? Why were creation order and roles never symbolized with head covering before? Since God had never been offended with various head covering of man and woman, except as He had prescribed for the priests, it is untenable that one's head was dishonored in the eyes of God.

ALLEGED THAT HEAD COVERING DEPICTS FEMININITY

Evidence for gender-specific headwear protocol during prayer and prophesying in the synagogue services is lacking. Scripture does not support that the presence or lack of head covering indicates gender.

ALLEGED HEAD COVERING IS A DEFENSE AGAINST FEMINISM

These Corinthians had failed to function according to the actual principles of headship. Headship precludes feminism. (discussed in chapter 5) Had they truly functioned according to the complimentary roles of man and woman, they would have recognized that both genders needed exactly the same covering to worship Him. (Gen.3:21)

Deborah Was Not A Feminist

Among the biblical illiterate today, Deborah would be considered a feminist. But this godly woman displayed her understanding of gender roles, when she deferred to Barak to lead Israel in battle. She honored the man's created leadership role. No mention is made of head covering.

Feminism Is Built on Self-Esteem

Despite the absence of a universal biblical mandate for head covering, commentaries link modern day feminism to the disregard of this custom.[19] But feminism emerged from the doctrine of self-esteem, where God-

---

[19] Jeremy Gardiner, *Head Covering*, p. 15-17

created roles, such as marriage and motherhood, were devalued. Deborah submitted to Barak because of who she was not what she wore.

Head Covering For Priests Was God Ordained

High Priests wore turbans in the administration of the sacrificial system. Other priests wore caps as they served in maintenance of the tabernacle. It is certain that the styles of these head coverings would not have confused men and women concerning the roles of men and women. God had designed the priestly wardrobe for males. Priests did not wear head covering to distinguish them from women.

ALLEGED PROTECTION FROM TEMPTATION

It is supposed that man is seduced by uncovered hair of women, yet this didn't seem to be an issue in the OT. But the Scriptures are instructive regarding differences between the clothing of the two genders.

> "While the costume of men and women were very similar, there was an easily recognizable distinction between the male and female attire of the Israelites, and accordingly the Mosaic Law forbids men to wear women's clothes and vice versa." [20] (De. 22:5)

God mandated that male and female be distinguished by clothing style. Failure to follow not only biblical admonition, but also God-given natural inclinations of men and women to indicate their sexuality by what they wear, is a sign of homosexuality. When man dresses according to his masculinity and woman dresses according to her femininity, they, by nature, depict their sex according to God's design. Both genders wore dresses in those days! Both genders covered their heads! But then, as now, the styles of man's and woman's clothing were tailored differently. Head covering for man would be masculine, and for woman, feminine.

So, to infer from 1 Cor. 11:1-16 that the presence or absence of a head covering indicated a crossover of sexual identity, is outside the bounds of Paul's context.[21] The biblical record indicates that men and women, wearing head covering at their discretion, did not cause a confusion of sexual identity. The OT forbids men and women to wear the same styles. This would also apply to head covering. (Deut. 22:5)

---

[20] Merrill. F. Unger, *Unger's Bible Dictionary*, p.277

[21] Mark Finney, *Honour, Head Coverings and Headship*, p. 44
https://www.sheffield.ac.uk/polopoly_fs/1.299952!/file/JSNT.pdf

Another commentator disallows culture-based speculations on head covering,

> "While each of the explanations are "creative" in attempting to find some societal connection for the use of head coverings, they are merely speculative and cannot be harmonized with history and Scripture. Darrel Bock, professor at Dallas Theological Seminary, states, "Suggestions that the presence or absence of a head covering was associated with prostitution, adultery, homosexuality, pagan worship, mourning, immodesty, etc.... often suffer from a lack of evidence..." The fact that these explanations widely differ from each other further betrays the fact that an obvious historical-cultural interpretation does not exist. Those who seek a cultural basis for Paul's instructions are unable to legitimately identify one."[22]

Descriptions of the social context of head covering by many commentators cannot be biblically substantiated. Most importantly, they miss the point that Paul specifically refers to the time of praying and prophesying only. If head covering protocol helped to protect believers from temptation, why should this only apply during the time of worship?

REVISING SCRIPTURE

Some conjecture that a principle need not be found in the OT to be valid. In other words, Paul was at liberty to dictate a new custom that had no foundation in the Law and the Prophets. It is argued that, though a uniform law concerning head coverings in prayer and prophesying did not exist in the OT, Paul was introducing a new moral law.

REVISING SCRIPTURE BY ADDITION

Jesus rebuked the Pharisees for transgressing the Law with added traditions. (Matt.15:3-9) They were teaching commandments of men, as doctrines. They had invented a law that absolved children from the obligations of the 4th commandment. If they dedicated a sum of money to God, they did not have to use it to take care of their parents if they called it 'Corban'. Paul warned Titus not to pay attention to Jewish fables and commandments of men. (Titus 1:14)

---

[22] David Phillips, *Covered Glory*, p.20, Though Phillips rightly observes unproven theories among commentators, he presumes imperatives in the text that do not exist.
http://www.coveredglory.com/uploads/3/0/5/2/30523312/coveredglory.pdf

Head Covering in Scripture

REVISING SCRIPTURE BY ABROGATING THE OT.

Commentators also subtract from Scripture by teaching a 'New Covenant Theology', that has replaced the Moral Covenant of the OT known as the Decalogue. They base this doctrine on the words of Jesus when He said, 'a new *kainos* commandment I give unto you, that you love one another.' (Jn. 13:34; Lev. 19:18) However, the love commandment existed in the OT. How then do we understand the words of Christ?

The word for 'new' (*kainos*) does not mean 'new' in respect of time. It denotes something to which one is unaccustomed or unused.[23] The disciples would not think of washing each other's feet. They even argued about who would be the greatest in Christ's kingdom. (Lk. 22:21-27) Christ was actually exhorting them, 'An unused commandment give I unto you.' By His own example, even as the King of Kings, He, rebuked them by stooping to wash their feet. The OT had left them plenty of instruction and examples of love. But the disciples were not 'accustomed' to this commandment. It was 'new' to them, not new to Scripture.

Neither did Christ imply that the Commandments had been abrogated in the Sermon on the Mount. In fact, Christ alluded to the 10th Commandment not to covet, when He taught the people that even to lust after a woman was to commit adultery. The standard for the knowledge of sin never changed from old to new testaments.

SUMMARY

The OT is cited by NT authors numerous times. NT verses repeat or amplify OT truth. (1 Thess.5:17, Rom. 12:10-14; 2 Thess.3:13; Col. 3:17, Mat. 6:19,20) If the NT violated existing instructions of doctrine and morality taught in the OT, it could not be inspired by God.

God always required that man repent of his sin, trust Christ as his Savior and grow by his knowledge of the word. (Psa.119:11) The NT has the special focus of revealing Christ as the fulfillment of OT prophecy. God's list of sins was the same before Christ, as they are after. The means of salvation and sanctification never changed. When outward expressions of worship were to be abrogated, there was no doubt. First, by Christ at the Lord's Table, then through the Apostles, it was made clear how religious tradition should be changed. (11:24-26)

If God was displeased with inappropriate headwear before Christ, the evidence would be found in the OT. In the absence of a censure for

---

[23] *Vine's Expository Dictionary of New Testament Words*

inappropriate headwear; dishonoring one's own head cannot be defined as sin. So, if headdress was not an issue in the OT, it follows that there must be another explanation for why an individual 'dishonors' his or her head. Since there was no general instruction for worship headwear in the OT, apostolic directives to the contrary would, at the very least, appear to add to scripture.

OT Scripture Of The Bereans

The Bereans set a wonderful example for every believer. When the Bereans heard that the Christ they had been waiting for had died and risen from the dead, they checked the OT Scriptures to see if this was so. (Ac.17:10-12) They didn't say, 'Let us ask the 'pastor.' They didn't stop to ask the synagogue president or a resident priest! Had the issue been the problem of head covering, they would have also searched the Scriptures intently for that answer. They had been anticipating prophecy to be fulfilled.

However, it appears that the 'normal' reading of Paul's instruction on head covering was that a new custom for worship was required. (1 Cor. 11:1-16) But is that the 'actual' reading? Had the Bereans heard about a head covering mandate, the Bereans would have checked the OT Scriptures.

3 Paul's Traditions

Paul challenged each believer to examine his life and follow him as he followed Christ. He exhorted them not to offend either the Jew or the Greek. (10:32-11:1) This church had become image conscious regarding leadership, wisdom and traditions. Yet, Paul had commended them for keeping the traditions he delivered to them. Some teach that Paul praised them for keeping a newly 'delivered' head covering tradition.[24] (11:17) If this were so, his word and example should support this view. What were Paul's traditions?

Optional Traditions

Despite Paul's impressive religious resume, his apostolic instructions precluded the continuing necessity of Jewish traditions such as circumcision, diet, and the Nazarite vow. Though no longer required, Paul continued to practice them as he saw fit.

The Rite Of Circumcision

Knowing that God had also saved Gentiles before Christ, the Apostles and elders at the Council of Jerusalem already had OT precedent for the reception of Gentiles, without the need for circumcision. (Ac. 15:14-17)

Abel, Enoch and Noah all preceded the rite of circumcision, yet are listed in Hebrews as men of faith. Jethro, Moses' father-in-law, was a priest of Midian, who rejoiced with Moses for all the good things God had done for Israel and offered sacrifices to God on their behalf. He was not a Jew. (Ex. 18:9-12) During Israel's captivity, through the witness of Daniel and his friends, Nebuchadnezzar, a Gentile king blessed and praised and exalted the God of heaven. He was a convert, but there is no reason to believe that he ever became a Jew! (Da.4:34-37) As saving faith was not dependent upon circumcision before Christ, neither was it necessary after.

However, for the sake of gospel ministry by Jews to Jews, Paul recommended circumcision. For this reason, Paul circumcised Timothy, whose mother was a Jewess. (Ac. 16:3; 1 Cor. 7:17-24)

---

[24] Jeremy Gardiner, *Head Coverings*, p. 20

NAZARITE TRADITION

Apparently, Paul also observed the Nazarite custom.

> ""Then the Lord spoke to Moses, saying, "Speak to the children of Israel and say to them: 'When <u>either a man or woman </u>consecrated an offering to take the vow of a Nazirite, to separate himself to the Lord...""" (Num. 6:1,2; NKJ, emphasis added)

The Nazarite vow was a Jewish self-imposed obligation. Women, as well as men, took this vow.

Secondly, the man or woman would vow not to cut his or her hair for a specified period of time.

> "Then the Nazarite shall shave his consecrated head at the door of the tabernacle of meeting, and shall take the hair from his consecrated head and put it on the fire which is on the sacrifice of the peace offering." (Nu. 6:18; NKJ)

If any Jews took the vow in the Corinthian assembly, the man's hair would be long when he completed his vow, and the woman's cut hair short when she made the vow. At the end of a specified period of time, the hair was cut and presented at the temple. (Num. 6:9, 18-19) Though there is some debate whether Paul had specifically taken a Nazarite vow, Paul had taken a vow where he, along with others, who also had taken a vow, went to the temple to have their heads shorn. (Acts. 18:18,19; 21:22-24)

SUMMARY

Paul purposed to glorify God in everything. (10:31; 11:1) In the past he had been 'exceedingly zealous for the traditions of his fathers'. But, keeping traditions just for the sake of prestige and recognition was antithetical to who he had become in Christ. (1 Cor. 4:8-13; Ga. 1:14) Yet, despite his inspired realization that the Jewish religious practices were no longer required, Paul himself continued to observe some of these past traditions for the sake of the Gospel. But, to impose one external religious head covering tradition would exacerbate existing divisions.

THE FELLOWSHIP TRADITION

Greeting family members with a hug is an ancient tradition. Laban embraced Jacob when he discovered that he was a relative. (Ge. 29:13) Esau embraced his brother Jacob. (Ge. 33:4) Joseph embraced and kissed

Paul's Traditions

his brother Benjamin. (Ge. 45:14) Joseph embraced and kissed his father Jacob. (Ge. 46:29) Jacob embraced and kissed Joseph's sons. (Ge. 48:10) Jesus also illustrated His own overwhelming welcome of a long lost son, by running to him, falling on his neck and kissing him. (Lk. 15:20)

Love was also expressed among friends. Sad to see Paul leave, the elders repeatedly embraced him. (Ac 20:37) Given the fact that the Jews considered the Gentiles unclean, it is particularly noteworthy that Paul and Peter command believers five times to greet one another with a 'holy' kiss. (Rom. 16:16; 1 Cor. 16:20; 2 Cor. 13:12; 1 Thess. 5:26; 1 Pet. 5:14)

'Greet' or 'salute', "signifies to draw to oneself." (Vine's Expository Dictionary) This verb, *aspazomai*, is also translated as 'embrace in Acts 20:1 and Heb. 11:13. It may be that when believers 'greeted' one another with a 'holy kiss', they may not have embraced. However, from the context of this verb, we must conclude that the 'holy kiss' was accompanied with a 'greeting' in word or with an embrace, or both. As believers naturally embraced members of their own family, Paul commands Jew and Gentile believers to embrace one another as members of the same spiritual family as the elders had, men with men and women with women. Fellowship among believers precludes social distancing.

REQUIRED 'DELIVERED' TRADITIONS

It is alleged that the tradition for which the Corinthians were praised was head covering. (11:2) However, as the narrative unfolds, it is apparent that the Corinthians were not keeping a head covering tradition. Paul had complimented them for keeping two mandated traditions, not just one.

There is some debate as to whether *paradoseis* should be translated 'instruction' or 'tradition'. Either view does not alter Paul's intent. Both baptism and the Lord's Table were commands or traditions from our Lord that Paul exhorted them to keep.

BAPTISM

Paul had faithfully delivered the teaching of baptism as Christ had commanded his disciples. (Matt. 28:19) Not only had they become attached to this tradition, regrettably, it had also become a status symbol based on who baptized them. (1:14-17) Indeed, they had kept the ordinance of baptism but because of their sectarianism, Paul was thankful that he had only baptized a few. (1:14) Their attitudes, notwithstanding, the Corinthians were keeping this tradition.

THE LORD'S TABLE

Likewise, Paul delivered to the church the tradition of the Lord's Table that Christ had established. (Matt.2:26-29; 1 Cor. 11:23) They had been observing this ordinance. (11:17-34). Yet, as they kept this tradition, he could not compliment them for how they kept it. (11:17) Some had been bringing food for this feast without sharing with those who had little or none. They had been ignoring the reason for the meal, celebrating an ordinance without discerning the Lord as their Head. (11:20)

SUMMARY

The Corinthians were only praised for keeping the ordinances, not for how they kept them. (11:2, 17-22) Elitists among them boasted about who baptized them. Some ignored the needs of others at the Lord's Table. Even in keeping these God-ordained traditions, God was dishonored.

Delivered by Paul, Baptism and the Lord's Table were traditions the church held to. Regarding the Lord's Table Paul explains that not only did he receive this from the Lord, but that he also delivered this tradition to them. (11:23) However, nothing in the text implies that Paul had received an ordinance from the Lord for worship head covering.

PAUL'S PURPOSE FOR TRADITION

Had there been any religious significance to head covering during corporate prayer and prophesying, the Apostles and elders would have come to a consensus on this matter as well. And, it is also certain that their decision would have been based on the OT.

Himself delivered from the self-righteous attainments of a Pharisee, Paul no longer demanded adherence to Jewish religious rites and traditions. The supposed introduction of another tradition by which Christians could and would judge one another is, therefore, untenable. Why would he endorse another tradition, such as head covering?

Apostolic traditions served to highlight the believer's fellowship with Christ and each other. Head covering expectations, as will be shown from Paul's text, only divided believers from one another.

4 Head Covering & Hair Traditions

Evidently, sources of conflict within the fellowship of believers were not limited to Jewish traditions, such as circumcision and dietary laws. Despite having no biblical mandate, the presence or lack of head covering had been another irritant during worship. (11:4,5) Unable to resolve this head covering dispute, unity in the Corinthian fellowship, their spiritual health and witness had been compromised.

A review of these customs in extra-biblical history, particularly as they pertain to the Roman, Greek and Jewish culture, does provide some vital context for the head covering strife in the Corinthian church.

SCHOLARSHIP CONFLICTS

Can secular history help us to know what the Corinthian head covering traditions were? Kevin Moore cites various sources having various views on head covering. [25] One says that Roman and Jewish men prayed with their heads covered while another states that there is almost no evidence that Greeks, Romans or Jews prayed with their head covered. One author states that all women always wore veils, while another stated that they were used in exceptional cases. Some state that Jewesses were always veiled in public, yet another stated that this was not considered an essential for every day.

Moore assumes an interpretation from 1 Corinthians 11, that the norm for men was to be uncovered and women to be covered, concluding that "some pagan religious practices may have deviated from the normal standards of decency, but this was not as universal as some have argued."[26] He concludes there was a generally accepted "norm" for head covering common to Romans, Greeks and Jews, that customs associated with pagan rituals are of little consequence to this study. But, does the evidence support his conclusion?

---

[25] Kevin L. Moore, *A Critical Analysis of 1 Corinthians* 11:2-16, 1996, Page 12,13
http://apologeticspress.org/user_file/A%20CRITICAL%20ANALYSIS%20OF%201%20CORINTHIANS%2011_2-16.pdf

[26] Ibid., Page 26, 27

In addition to the Greek influence, the mingling populace of the Roman Empire also contributed to a variety of customs.

> "It should be borne in mind that ancient Greece was not a monolithic culture: customs varied from city to city in Greece, and the customs of Sparta are often mentioned as being peculiar, different from those of Athens and other cities." [27]

Despite scholarly differences on the custom of head coverings and hair lengths, especially as they relate to Paul's admonition to the church in Corinth, it must be admitted that Moore's "normal" does not exist. Simply, traditions of 'decency' are not the same in every culture.

HEAD COVERING TRADITIONS

This brief survey of head covering customs will focus on the different practices between men and women among the Romans, Greeks and Jews.

ROMAN MEN

Roman priests covered their heads in religious ceremonies. [28] Liturgically required head coverings, for Roman men in Corinth, can be documented for centuries before and after Christ. [29] Plutarch, a contemporary of Paul, asks a rhetorical question,

> "Why is it that when the Romans worship the gods, they cover their heads, but when they meet any of their fellow-men, worthy of honor, if they happen to have the toga over the head, they uncover?"[30]

This only implicates the Roman custom for how they worshipped. Literary evidence documents that the normative practice for pious Roman men in worship was to cover their head. Archaeological discoveries, including literary documents, unmistakably indicate that the common Roman liturgical practice for men was to cover the head. [31]

---

[27] Michael Marlowe, *Headcovering Customs of the Ancient World, An Illustrated Survey.* P.4
https://www.wednesdayintheword.com/resources/Marlowe-HeadcoveringCustoms.pdf

[28] Ibid., P. 5.

[29] Mark Finney, *Honour, Head Coverings and Headship:* 1Corinthians 2:11-16 in its Social Context, c.2010, P.37
https://www.sheffield.ac.uk/polopoly_fs/1.299952!/file/JSNT.pdf

[30] Ibid., P.39,40

[31] Ibid., P. 36, 37

Head Covering & Hair Traditions 21

ROMAN WOMEN

Women wore head covering for various reasons. Some say that the veil was a sign of subjection, to them it was also a 'badge of honor' and 'sexual reserve'. Among respectable women, head covering denoted that she was not available and to approach her could risk a confrontation with the man of her life.[32] A woman's head covering signaled that she was not to be propositioned, yet, the absence of a head covering indicated availability for marriage.[33]

Though data is somewhat ambiguous concerning Roman women attending religious ceremonies, it appears certain that women involved in sacerdotal functions covered their heads.[34] Some believe that every woman not wearing a head covering was promiscuous, yet ancient evidence indicates that respectable Roman women would appear in public without a head covering.[35] Women had their own personal reasons for wearing or not wearing a head covering.

GREEK MEN

Greek men, on the other hand, did not ordinarily worship their gods with anything on their head.[36] A. T. Robertson states that both Greek men and women remained bareheaded in public prayer.[37] Ancient pictorials and various literary sources indicate that the Greek practice of both men and women for prayer and libation was to keep the head uncovered.[38]

GREEK WOMEN

Biblical commentators have asserted that only Greek women of ill repute did not wear head coverings. Marlowe states that,

> "Many scholars now maintain that although Greek women certainly did wear head coverings at times, and probably more often than not in public, there is no good reason to think that

---

[32] Ibid., P. 40, 41

[33] Ibid., P.36, 40

[34] Ibid., P. 38

[35] Michael Marlowe, *Headcovering Customs of the Ancient World*, An Illustrated Survey. P.7
https://www.wednesdayintheword.com/resources/Marlowe-HeadcoveringCustoms.pdf

[36] Ibid. P. 2

[37] *Robertson Word Pictures in the New Testament*, Please see commentary on 1 Cor. 11:4
https://www.studylight.org/commentaries/eng/rwp/1-corinthians-11.html

[38] Jeffrey W. Hamilton, *Images of Head Coverings During Worship*, 'Greek Worship'
http://www.lavistachurchofchrist.org/LVarticles/ImagesOfHeadCoveringsDuringWorship.htm

Greek women were under some compulsion to cover their heads in public. The idea that immoral women were recognized as such by the absence of a head covering has no basis at all in ancient evidence."[39]

Some Greek cults priestesses are depicted as presenting offerings without head coverings and did not always appear covered in public.[40] Head covering for women was optional at religious ceremonies but was expected of women who participated in sacerdotal functions.[41] Apparently, pagan Greek women did not always cover their heads when they worshipped.[42] Greek women were known to worship with their head uncovered, but with tiaras or leaf chaplets in their hair.

JEWISH MEN

Some claim that all Jewish men always prayed with their heads covered, but this view cannot be supported from history. Indeed, the priests wore caps in the maintenance of the tabernacle and the High Priests wore a turban in the administration of the sacrifices. So, it is likely that converted priests would have carried this OT temple tradition into the corporate worship of Christ. (Ac. 6:7) But, the general expectation of a prayer shawl or tallit for men did not come into existence until the third century.[43]

JEWISH WOMEN

And, it is held that there is evidence that Jewish women covered their heads not only for prayer but also for going out in public. But, as shown in chapter 2, except for the priesthood, no custom for either man or woman in regards to head covering for worship was mandated.

Mary, the sister of Lazarus, anointed the feet of Jesus with expensive ointment, then wiped his feet with her hair at the house of Simon, the leper. (Matt. 26:7; Jn. 12:1-9) At this public event, where most present were men, Mary did not feel it necessary to be covered. Secondly, she worshiped Christ with her head uncovered. It is noteworthy that she was

---

[39] Michael Marlowe, *Headcovering Customs of the Ancient World*, An Illustrated Survey, P. 3
https://www.wednesdayintheword.com/resources/Marlowe-HeadcoveringCustoms.pdf

[40] Ibid., P. 4,5

[41] Mark Finney, *Honour, Head Coverings and Headship*: 1Corinthians 2:11-16 in its Social Context, c.2010, P. 37
https://www.sheffield.ac.uk/polopoly_fs/1.299952!/file/JSNT.pdf

[42] Michael Marlowe, *Headcovering Customs of the Ancient World*, An Illustrated Survey, P. 4
https://www.wednesdayintheword.com/resources/Marlowe-HeadcoveringCustoms.pdf

[43] Ibid., P. 8

Head Covering & Hair Traditions

not criticized for her apparent lack of 'modesty', but for having 'wasted' the ointment.

SUMMARY

From historical data, it is evident that no single practice was required or considered "normal" for men and women pagan worshippers in first century Corinth. After his observations of Roman and Greek liturgical head wear customs, Bruce Terry concludes that,

> "The evidence seems to indicate that in the first century among the Romans, both men and women covered their heads at worship, while among the Greeks, both men and women uncovered their heads when they worshiped."[44]

Despite the different views among the scholars regarding first century head covering customs, we can be certain that these customs were not homogenous, either socially or religiously. It is clear that Romans, Greeks and Jews practiced different head covering customs in worship. Had Paul been truly concerned with the lack of woman's head covering, surely he would have counseled women with "braided hair" to wear a head covering. Rather, he exhorts them to be modest. (1 Tim. 2:9)

With a mixture of Romans, Greeks and Jews in the Corinthian church, this background provides additional context for the real cause of strife.

CUSTOMS PERTAINING TO HAIR

Paul's exhortation contrasts head covering with short hair and implies that some women among them may have had their hair cut short, perhaps even shaved.

DID A WOMAN'S SHORT HAIR SIGNAL SEXUAL PERVERSION?

Some scholars associate extra-biblical incidents of prevailing degrading sexual passions in Greek and Roman society with women who had short hair, signaling their desire to be superior to man and even to change sex.[45] If hair length always identifies a lesbian, Paul's admonition would have a general application, not just for corporate 'praying and prophesying'. And, because women with long hair are also lesbians, acceptable worship

---

[44] *Aspects of Culture at Corinth*, Bruce Terry, See 'Head Coverings'
http://bible.ovc.edu/terry/dissertation/2_4-aspects.htm

[45] Matthew Henry, *Matthew Henry's Commentary on the Whole Bible*, Vol. VI, P. 561

cannot be known by outward appearance. Regulating hair length according to gender would not regulate homosexuality.

DID A WOMAN'S SHORT HAIR SIGNIFY PAGAN WORSHIP?

Some interpreters reason that a thousand priestesses who served as prostitutes in the worship of Aphrodite had their heads shorn. But scholars have raised serious doubts as to the extent and even the reality of cult prostitution in Corinth. Baugh contends with Strabo and other scholars on this issue,

> "And even if we were to accept Strabo's testimony that Corinth did have cult prostitution in the seventh century BC - which cannot be automatically granted - there is good reason to have serious doubts that it survived into the first century AD. Greek Corinth, as is well known, was destroyed by L. Mummius in 146 BC (e.g. Strabo 8.6.23), and re-founded in 44 BC as a Roman colony by Julius Caesar with a distinctly Roman character. Hence, as David Gill observes, "It is right for both classical archaeologists and New Testament scholars to stress the Roman nature of the city which was visited by Paul in the first century AD."[13] Or as the second-century mythographer and travel-writer Pausanias puts it: "Not one of the Corinthians of antiquity still lives in Corinth; instead there are colonists sent from Rome" (2.1.2). What this means for us is a presumption that the cult practices of ancient Greek Corinth had been radically altered by the *Romanitas* of its new population. And this is what Pausanias reports: "Since the Romans devastated Corinth and the ancient Corinthians perished, the old local sacrifices are no longer a tradition" (2.3.6)."[46]

Not all scholars believe that the Greek temple of Aphrodite worship had been restored to its former glory. It had been a great Greek city, but in Paul's day, the Romans were rebuilding it. Evidence, showing Corinth to have risen to its former proliferation of cult prostitution, is lacking. Murphy O'Connor believes that sacred prostitution was never a Greek custom.[47] Thus, linking a woman's short hair to pagan worship, is untenable.

---

[46] S.M. Baugh, *Cult Prostitution in New Testament Ephesus*, A Reappraisal, Journal of the Evangelical Theological Society, 1999. Section II Strabo And Corinth
https://biblicalstudies.org.uk/article_ephesus_baugh.html

[47] Ibid.

WHAT ELSE DID SHORT HAIR SIGNIFY?

In the Roman-Greco context, women typically uncovered their head during a time of mourning. The Roman women would unbind their hair and the Greek women would cut their hair short.[48] With a reference to Plutarch, Bruce Terry also affirms the custom of Greek women cutting their hair off in times of mourning.[49]

God 'hired' Assyria to shave Israel and disgrace him. Israel was called to repentance with sackcloth and baldness, but they ignored their God and celebrated instead. (De.21:12,13; Isa. 7:20;15:2; 22:12) Micah prophesies that the children would be taken captive, and therefore, should cut of all their hair and mourn now. (Mic.1:16)

Also, in the Jewish context, shaving of the head was a sign of grief. (Job. 1:20; Jer. 7:29; 16:6) And, as discussed in the previous chapter, both men and women would enter into the Nazarite vow, which necessitated the cutting of hair

SUMMARY

Eating sacrificed meat was *exclusively* associated with paganism, and for that reason Paul exhorted believers to refrain from eating it, **if** it might offend new believers. However, shorn hair did not *exclusively* indicate pagan worship or sexual perversion. Since it was also indicative of shame, grief or a vow, it is unreasonable to propose that this would disqualify anyone from corporate prayer. Depending on the circumstance, these different customs were appropriate.

CONCLUDING SUMMARY

Head covering customs differed primarily according to Greek, Roman and Jewish culture, and religion. It is particularly important to emphasize that the pagan Greeks and Romans usually observed opposite head covering customs in their worship. This presents some additional hurdles to justify Paul's supposed mandate to regulate head coverings and hair. If Paul ruled in favor of the Greeks, who generally did not cover their heads in worship, then the Roman converts might feel their worship was inadequate. And, conversely if Paul ruled in favor of the Roman men, who

---

[48] Mark Finney, *Honour, Head Coverings and Headship*: 1Corinthians 2:11-16 in its Social Context, c.2010, P.38
https://www.sheffield.ac.uk/polopoly_fs/1.299952!/file/JSNT.pdf

[49] Bruce Terry, *Aspects of Culture at Corinth*, Head Coverings
http://bible.ovc.edu/terry/dissertation/2_4-aspects.htm

covered their heads for worship, then Greek converts might feel uncomfortable in their worship. This is further complicated with Jewish priests who may have been inclined to cover while other Jewish men might not. With different head covering traditions deemed to show God 'respect' during 'prayer and prophesying', the supposition that some were compelled to discard theirs, becomes much harder to defend. As stated previously, to mandate one custom, would have exacerbated the strife already troubling the church on this and other issues.

Neither was the lack of head covering, and even the lack of hair, an indication of prostitution. Regarding shorn hair, it is clear from Scripture that Jews cut their hair for reasons having nothing to do with paganism and sexual identification. In fact, among the Greeks and Romans, short hair was also a means of communicating grief. Would Paul disallow a custom that was a means of expressing their grief?

Diverse inhabitants with diverse cultures naturally observed different social and religious customs. Excluding the principle of moderation, there is no hint that a believer's worship was enhanced by the quantity of hair or the presence or lack of head covering.

Paul now informs the church regarding the principles of headship.

5 The Principles of Headship

Gripped by pious sectarianism, these Corinthian professing believers had not properly understood their relation with God and one another. So, just before he exposes yet another divisive distraction, he introduces another doctrine. Having complimented them on remembering traditions he had taught them; Paul now transitions to another subject. (11:3) The adversative conjunction 'but', (*de* :- on the other hand) indicates that Paul was about to change the subject.

On other matters of spiritual growth, Paul had repeatedly asked them, 'do you not know?' [50] In this instance, he skips the question and simply states that he wanted them to know the doctrine of headship that they could have discovered in the OT. (11:3a)

> "But I want you to know that the head of every man is Christ, the head of woman is man, and the head of Christ is God." (11:3, NKJV)

The Scriptures have much to teach us about headship.

SUPPOSED MEANINGS OF 'HEAD'

Commentaries, in my view, are in large part responsible for an unbiblical understanding of this text. It is assumed that the 'head' of anything means to be the ruler, the master, or the boss. Ultimately, the Scriptures must serve as its own lexicon.

DOES 'HEAD' MEAN SUBJUGATION?

Commentators have inferred subjugation from this doctrine that the context does not support. Headship has been conflated with subordination and inferiority.

Incorrect Inferences

Commenting on the phrase 'and the head of the woman is the man', Barnes writes,

---

[50] Paul repeatedly addressed the ignorance of the Corinthians with, 'know ye not?' (3:16; 5:6; 6:2,3,9,15,16,19; 9:13,24)

> "The sense is that she is subordinate to him, and in all circumstances – in her demeanor, her dress, her conversation, in public and the family circle – should recognize her subordination to him."[51]

There is nothing in this verse about subjugation or subordination or dominion![52]

Otherwise sound in soteriology and anthropology, commentators have vented negative attitudes regarding women. Note John Gill's reasoning for why the man is the head of the woman.

> "The man is first in order in being, was first formed, and the woman out of him, who was made for him, and not he for the woman, and therefore must be head and chief; as he is also with respect to his <u>superior gifts</u> and excellencies, as strength of body, <u>and endowments of mind,</u> <u>whence the woman is called the weaker vessel</u> . . ."[53] (emphasis added)

If headship implies that the woman is less intelligent than man, then Christ must also be less intelligent than God. (11:3)

DOES HEADSHIP IMPLY GOVERNANCE?

Lexicon definitions of 'head' are 'chief', 'ruler', 'supreme', etc. From these it is inferred that the authority of the 'head' is autocratic, that man is the chief of woman. Since God is not the king or chief of Jesus, this definition cannot explain the relation of man and woman.

Headship Precludes Governance

Commentaries have failed to distinguish between two entirely different concepts – governance and headship.

Headship implies a preexisting unity evidenced by willing and eager compliance between two persons for mutual benefit and glory. Governance, on the other hand, requires coercion to gain and maintain dominion. People may well be compliant but are not necessarily unified. At creation, which Paul references, man was not governing the woman! Governance came as the result of the Fall, not headship! (11:8,9)

---

[51] *Albert Barnes Notes on the Whole Bible*, 1 Cor. 11:3, (see studylight.org)

[52] *Cambridge Greek Testament for Schools and Colleges*, says that 'head' "has the idea of dominion". Ellicott says "Christ is subordinate to the Father." Christ submitted to the Father, He was obedient to the Father, <u>but</u> He was <u>not</u> subordinate to the Father.

[53] John Gill, *John Gill's Exposition of the Whole Bible*, (See Studylight.org)

The Principles of Headship

Does 'Head' Imply Prominence?

Some argue that the Greek word for "head" in the NT means 'prominent', pertaining to the husband in the "patriarchal social structure of Paul's day."[54] Man is 'prominent' as the head but he is not superior to woman. However, the essential work of Son is more prominent than the Father, who is the Head.

Does 'Head' Imply Source?

Others argue for the meaning of 'source'.[55] In verse 8, Paul reminds the church that the woman was made from man. He was the passive source of woman. Yet, after creation, without woman, man would cease to exist, since man comes also by the woman. (11:11) Both man and woman could claim to be the source of the other. To argue for headship on this basis, is therefore also irrelevant.

The Bible Is Our Lexicon

The meaning of 'head' must be determined by both immediate and the broader scriptural context. Written in the present indicative active, they are made aware of a fact, an unchanging precept,

> "But I would have you know, that the head of every man is Christ, and the head of the woman is the man; and the head of Christ is God." (11:3, KJV)

God, Christ, man and woman are the subjects of this verse as it pertains to headship. Headship is a present, intrinsic reality, not only in the righteous Deity, but also in sinful humanity.

What is Paul's Meaning of 'Head'?

What then are the real terms of biblical headship?

The Greek word *kephale*, like English has other meanings beside the physical head of a body. According to Thayer's, 'head' also may be a metaphor for a supreme, chief, prominent person master or lord. But, how can these definitions possibly apply in this context?

As part of the body, 'head' has an organic connotation. A mechanical or forced subjugation by one person over another supersedes the physical

---

[54] Alan F. Johnson, *A Review of the Scholarly Debate on the Meaning of "Head"*, p.54
https://biblicalstudies.org.uk/pdf/ashland_theological_journal/41-1_035.pdf

[55] Liddell Scott Greek English Lexicon, Seventh Edition, p.801
https://archive.org/stream/greekenglishlex00liddrich#page/800/mode/2up

nuance of the word. Paul's use of the word 'head' must refer to a natural disposition to coordinate with others as if they were members of his own body. It's the natural alignment of one mind with another, not over another. Paul's use of 'head' is an organic metaphor illustrative of a coordinated unforced compliance of one mind with another.

Additional context, shows how the Scriptures is our lexicon.

THE THREE 'HEADSHIPS'

Paul identifies three relationships pertaining to headship. (11:3) The first headship relation is without flaw in principle and practice. But due to the Fall, the other two relations are right in principle but flawed in practice.

- God the Father is the Head of Christ. (Jn. 17:3-5)
- Christ is the Head of man.
- Man is the head of woman.

If, as lexicons define 'head', means king, supreme, serious conflicts arise with Scripture in its description of the godhead. Is God really the king of Christ? Is God supreme and Christ second? Is God the president and the Son, the vice-resident? Is man the king of woman?

GOD IS HEAD OF CHRIST

Christ came to do the will of the Father. (Matt. 26:42; Jn. 5:30) This implies that Christ recognized the Father as having authority. Feeling anguish in the Garden of the wrath of God He would have to endure, Christ did pray that this cup would be removed. Nevertheless, He wanted the Father's will to be done. (Lk.22:42) He submitted to the Father's will. But did He submit to the Father as a subject of a king?

Christ desired the will of God. (Jn. 17:11,21,24) In fact, he considered the trust that God laid before Him a joy! (Heb.12:2) Submitting to headship authority was a joy for Christ.

CHRIST IS HEAD OF MAN

Christ also said that He had the <u>authority</u> to lay down his life and take it up again of His own accord. (Jn.10:18) When He commissioned His disciples, Jesus claimed that he had been given authority in heaven and on earth. (Matt. 28:18-20; Jn. 20:21) Headship authority precludes competition. As Christ submitted to the Father, this also afforded the capacity for a regenerate man's autonomous submission to Christ.

Man is Head Of Woman

Paul writes that Christ is the Head of every man, not just the married man or the saved man. He makes no exceptions regarding headship. (1 Cor. 5; 15:2) Both the immediate and broader context does not exclude the unmarried man or woman. Had Paul intended only married man and woman, a sizeable portion of the congregation would have no 'head'. And Paul himself, being unmarried, would then not be 'head' of woman. Therefore, the headship precept transcends the marriage bond.

Paul alludes to man's headship when he states that the woman was made for man. (11:9) More will be discussed in a later chapter why feminists misunderstand this statement. But for now, it should be emphasized that this is not about a master/servant relation. Even Christ, who was not a created being, did the work the Father sent Him to do. The godhead is our headship prototype.

Summary

Unfortunately, many commentaries fail to distinguish between headship and governance. Had the Holy Spirit intended to teach us governance instead of headship, He could have used words such as 'king', 'master', 'ruler' or 'sovereign' or 'governor'.

As the relation of God the Father and God the Son are dependent upon one another, so also is the relation of man and woman. As God the Son or God the Father cannot exist without the other, neither can man or woman.

Despite the sin of man and woman, Christ is still the Head of man, and man is still the head of woman. Divine headship is the only perfect example to guide man and woman to relate to their respective heads in overcoming their head covering conflicts.

The Precept Of Headship

It is our task then to ascertain the unique features of headship pertaining to the three relations above. Though sin has compromised man's relation to his Head and woman's relation to hers, man's status as the head of woman has not been abrogated. Having created man and woman in the image of God, the precept of headship is still human reality.

What then, should believers know about His perfect headship, the image of God, in which man and woman were created?

HEADSHIP IS GROUNDED IN RIGHTEOUSNESS

Having the same holy and righteous nature, it is impossible for the members of the Trinity to come to different conclusions regarding right and wrong. (Jn. 17:25; 2 Tim. 4:8)

HEADSHIP DEPICTS A CREATED NATURAL RELATIONSHIP

God describes the relation between two members of the godhead in human terms of Father and Son. The Father/Son anthropomorphism indicates an indissoluble bond, where one is naturally the head of the other. God is the Head of Christ.

God did not create man or woman to be 'head' of animals, but to have dominion over them. Headship pertains to life of the same kind and therefore man could only be head of woman, because she is of the same flesh. (11:8) The Son is exclusively the 'express' image of God, but, man and woman having been uniquely created in the image of God were designed to depict divine headship. (11:7; Heb.1:2)

HEADSHIP IS UNIQUE

The creation of human life is unique. Male and female of all animal life was created of the 'same kind' but not from the same flesh. Christ is the Head of man. Woman was taken from the rib of man, and thus mankind is not only of one kind, but also of one flesh.

HEADSHIP NECESSITATES ROLES

Headship presupposes different work. The roles of the Father and the Son are different. (Jn.17:4) The Son did **not** send the Father to do a specific work. (Jn.4:34) The Father had given words for the Son to say to His elect. (Jn.17:6,8) The role of the Father was to dispense the work; the role of Son was to do the work He was assigned to do for our salvation.

Man's And Woman's Roles Are Instinctive

When society or a household is endangered, do men call upon the women to defend them while they go for cover with the children? No! When threatened, man instinctively knows that he is to protect women and children. Paul shows this same principle when he compares husband and wife with Christ and the church. (Eph.5:23)

Man's And Woman's Roles Are Different

Similarly, the roles of man and woman are also different, not interchangeable, but equally important. (11:9) Eve was uniquely made by God **to be** a suitable helper. (Gen.2:18) Her role is inherent. God did not

The Principles of Headship

give Adam a list of things for Eve to do, nor did He give Adam the additional responsibility of defining what Eve's help should look like. Eve would instinctively understand how to expedite the work specific to her role. Man doesn't need to help her **to know** how to be a suitable helper.

When confronted with conflicts in the church, the 'apostles and elders' came together to discuss the matter in question. The overall guidance and leadership of His people is the role of men, especially older, mature men. (Ac. 15:6) Instruction of men and women when assembled together is the role of men. Older, mature women were to be teachers of younger women. Although more and more women are assuming 'church' leadership, this is contrary to the role in which they had been created.

Man's And Woman's Roles Are Complimentary

The Son was not under the governance of His Father. Likewise, when God created Eve, Adam was not given dominion <u>over</u> her. Both man and woman were charged with the responsibility of governance over all that He created, not each other. (Gen. 1:26) Because the woman was created as helper, not slave, her work in that role <u>would not be identical</u> to man's, but complimentary. Differing roles entail different work, not competitive work. Both man and woman have important and essential roles to fulfill. The role of God, the Son, in saving us was different than the work of God, the Father, yet both roles were essential and therefore complimentary.

HEADSHIP DENOTES HARMONY

Christ had a mind of his own. Paul says, "Let this mind be in you which was also in Christ Jesus." Christ, not the Father, made of Himself of no reputation, yet He had no feelings of competition with the Father. (Phil. 2:5-9) On His own accord, Christ submitted to the will of the Father. Independent and autonomous, Christ amicably yielded to the Father. As the Father's headship facilitates the mind of Christ, so also should man's headship facilitate the mind of woman. Different than mere appendages of a body, headship necessitates the conscious and intelligent association and coordination of two minds. Headship, then, is one means by which <u>immanent</u> unity of two persons is displayed.

HEADSHIP DENOTES EQUALITY

God as 'Head' of Christ does not imply that God has greater power than Christ. Being God Himself, Christ did not consider it robbery to think of Himself as with God. (Phil. 2:5,6; Jn.8:58) Similarly, man's headship does not imply superiority.

God's headship of Christ is not due to deficient or insufficient knowledge. The Son's willing obedience to the Father was not necessitated by ignorance; His knowledge was as complete and as infallible as the Father's. As God the Father, and God the Son are equal, so also are man and woman.

HEADSHIP DENOTES INTERDEPENDENCE

As God the Father does not exist without the Son, so also man does not exist without the woman. (11:8) As the Head of Christ, God was not more knowledgeable, more powerful, wiser, more loving, etc. and as head of woman, neither is man. Christ's autonomous submission to the Father was not indicative of an inferior status!

Headship was not a means to strengthen a 'weaker vessel'. Headship is an intrinsic aspect of divinity. Eternally preexistent, neither the Father or the Son was the cause of the other, therefore, one cannot exist without the other. Headship is the means by which God the Father and Son together perform their will and show their power and wisdom.

Similarly, Paul explains that man and woman do not exist independently. Though man was created first and woman second, man must concede that he would cease to exist without woman. (11:11,12) Since creation, every man's existence is dependent on his mother, a woman. Both man and woman are necessary for the continuing existence of humanity and thus interdependent.

HEADSHIP FACILITATES AUTONOMY

Christ was not subjugated by God, to do the will of the Father. God the Father sent His Son; He did not coerce His Son. (Jn. 3:16,17) Jesus prayed, "O My Father, if it is possible, let this cup pass from Me; nevertheless, not as I will, but as You *will*." (Mt. 26:39, NKJV)

Jesus had a "will" and the Father had a "will", one demonstrating His voluntary, autonomous submission to the other. Christ's obedience was based on the same knowledge as the Father. (Phil. 2:5-10) "Having become", in Phil. 2:8, is in the middle voice indicating that compliance to the will of the Father was initiated by Christ and completed by Christ.

What would we think of a Savior who said, 'I died for you because the Father governed Me to the point where I was forced to'? Of course not! It is amazing that "for the joy that was set before Him, He endured the cross, despising the shame." (Heb.12:2) How good it is to know that despite the horrendous suffering He would bear in taking on the guilt and shame of our sin, as he faced the wrath of God, He did it gladly! Jesus never ever implied that the 'Father made me do it.' So, as two of the three persons of the godhead, each exercised His autonomy according to His role. Personal autonomy precludes governance. The Father did not govern Jesus. The Father did not subjugate Christ to do his will! Biblical headship precludes coercion or governance of any kind. This unexcelled example of submission of one member of the godhead to another is a sign of the love between them, not a sign of weakness or inferiority.

Authority Does Not Squelch Autonomy

Christ's own example indicates that authority does not presume the response of an automaton. There is no evidence that Jesus would have to ask God to still the wind and calm the sea. He did not have to check with His Father to gain permission to forgive someone's sin. As a Person of the Godhead, Christ is not a remotely controlled robot.

Woman's Autonomy Is Not Rebellion

Created as an autonomous, suitable helper for Adam, she is not part of man's dominion, nor was she to serve man as her master, lord, king or ruler, but as a suitable helper, who could discern how her work should be expedited. (Gen. 1:28; 2:22-24)

HEADSHIP FUNCTIONS BY CONSENSUAL AUTHORITY

Of course, authority is another function essential to headship. But, what kind of authority? The Godhead must be the standard.

Authority is Not Dictatorial

The authority of headship is not imposed. If authority becomes dictatorial, it no longer functions according to the precepts of headship. Indeed, governments are appointed by God to maintain order, even by the authoritarian imposition of law. But biblical headship is not governance. It does not impose laws.

God had granted permission to both man and woman to have dominion over the earth. (Gen.1:26-28) But man was not granted permission to have dominating authority over woman.

Authority is Not Hierarchal

The Father is the Head of Christ, yet one is not the sovereign over the other. But as 'the head of every man is Christ', is Christ not our Sovereign? (11:3) Is He not also our King? Indeed! However, since man is denoted as head of woman and God is not the king of Christ, this context precludes regal authority within the godhead. The response to a King is different that one's response to our Head.

Authority is Limited

Man's Head is exclusively Christ. Other men or women have no right to intercept Jesus' perfect headship authority of every man. Taken in the fellowship context in which this precept was given, 'every man' is to be individually guided by his Head, not popular opinion.

How would it ever be possible to get a group of men to agree on every matter, head covering notwithstanding? Imposed uniformity is a deadly virus that has infected Christian fellowships. The imposition of religious rules for headwear and the like is to violate the precept of headship.

Two of Jesus' disciples made a claim for governing authority with Christ. (Matt.20:20-26) Jesus told them that 'it shall not be so among you.' Headship rules out mediatory authority over others.

HEADSHIP DESIRES COMMUNICATION

Jesus manifested His name to those who were given to Him by the Father. (Jn. 17:7,8) The Son communicated to the Apostles the words that were given to Him by the Father. The Son talked to the Father; He didn't talk to Himself. (Jn. 17:6-8) Thus, headship is communicative.

Before the Fall, Adam demonstrated his headship by telling Eve exactly what God told him regarding eating the forbidden fruit. Headship requires the exchange of correct information. The Holy Spirit has given us His word by which man and woman can confirm if Christ, man's Head, is being followed. (14:37)

HEADSHIP EXALTS BOTH PERSONS

Our Lord prayed that His Father would glorify Him so He could glorify the Father. God's ultimate purpose was that both the Father and the Son would be glorified. (Jn. 17:1-5) True headship is not satisfied with exclusive glory. Divine headship glorifies the Father and the Son.

Despite the knowledge that He would face the Father's wrath for our sin, Christ also knew that this would redound ultimately for the glory of both. (Jn.17:1) At Jesus' baptism and transfiguration, the Father announced from heaven that He was well pleased with His Son. (Matt. 3:17; 17:5) The Son was to give eternal life to as many as the Father had given Him. The Father received glory for the plan and the Son received glory for the work of redemption. Mutual glory is indispensable to the function of God's headship of Christ.

The Principles of Headship

Summary

This brief appraisal delineates biblical headship as the knowledgeable, willing, discerning, and autonomous submission to the will of another for a mutually desired purpose and benefit. Since the inherent intention of the Father and Son is to glorify one another, it is impossible for the will of each to clash. As the Father exercised His authority on behalf of Christ to redound for the glory of both, so also is man to exercise his authority for the glory of both himself and woman. Though man's Head is always right and woman's head isn't, divine headship can be depicted as man and woman commend one another. Only when united in one purpose can man and woman practice the headship precept, as God did.

A Review of Headship

The following summary highlights some features of headship discussed to this point. Headship helps believers to understand...

- the basis for unity.
- that differences are not equal to division.
- that man's head is Christ, not man.
- that man's authority is Christ alone.
- that true authority is leading.
- that godly authority does not coerce.
- that godly authority is influential.
- that it is not subjugation of woman.
- that man is not a CEO.
- the voluntary compliance of one will to another.
- God at Creation and at the Cross.
- that one role is not more important than another.
- that woman is autonomous in her God-given role.
- that woman is safe guarded by Christ's headship.
- how praise of each other is facilitated.

The Godhead must be our example for leading and submission. But how does this apply to the Corinthian church?

Corinthian Headship Application

The Holy Spirit intentionally placed this doctrine as an introduction to the behavioral problems of head covering and the Lord's Table. False notions of authority had deflected the Corinthians from a scriptural understanding of the relation of man and woman to one another, and to

God. From the doctrine of headship, we can begin to postulate a few possible scenarios how this precept was not practiced.

1. Man tried to dominate other men.
2. Women may have tried to assume man's speaking role. (14:34)
3. Man may have tried to dictate customs for worship.
4. Man had not submitted to Christ, his Head, by exceeding what had been written. (4:6)
5. Man had substituted to other men in place of Christ. He forfeited his right to personal autonomy by thoughtlessly yielding to human wisdom. (1:20,21) They had introduced outward Pharisaical regulations having the appearance of godliness.
6. Woman had failed to recognize her autonomy to refuse to obey unbiblical regulation. Paul said, 'follow me as I follow Christ.'
7. Woman had failed to voluntarily yield to man's headship where it was not in conflict with Christ's headship of man.
8. Man had failed the practice of headship, thinking he is intellectually superior to woman.
9. Man and woman had become competitive, thus failing to exalt or compliment the other.

The Corinthian believers had obscured the headship precept. Having failed to understand the distinguishing roles of man and woman, harmony and unity among them was compromised.

SUMMARY

Only in the godhead do we find leading and following perfectly reciprocated with a natural, conscious, willing compliance of Christ to the Father. Created in the image of God, mankind has the potential to practice this principle.

Christ, as the Head of man, precludes any other man or woman as the head of man. Similarly, since man is head of woman, she cannot be head of another man or woman. Yet, it is vital for woman to know that biblical headship precludes error, that is, it never leads one into sin. She has the right to know Scripture in order to heed Paul's admonition to 'follow me as I follow Christ.' This liberty to independently follow Christ is not exclusive to man. (11:1) The same rights given to man to know and follow Christ, also belong to woman.

Despite their failures, Paul informs them of this defining, perennial principle of headship. (1:12,13; 11:3). Though the functions and features

The Principles of Headship

of headship were not evident in the lives of some of these believers, it was nonetheless a nonnegotiable reality.

Headship Is An Essential Principle.

The principle of headship naturally facilitates how man and woman together can accomplish difficult tasks, yet still maintain fellowship. Indifference to the doctrine of headship negatively impacts the spiritual growth of believers. In the case of the Corinthians' spiritual walk, they needed to understand the principles of headship to help them navigate past yet another hazard to their fellowship with Christ and one another.

Headship Is Not A Command

But there is no command in this verse. (11:3) Paul only enunciates a principle, a present reality. Christ is the Head of man whether he realizes it or not, whether he fails or succeeds.

CONCLUDING DEFINITIONS OF HEADSHIP

Having summarized some features of true headship as revealed in the Godhead and required by God for man, the following definitions are offered as a guide to our understanding of biblical teaching on headship.

Headship Of God Defined

True headship is the exclusive immanent right of the Father to lead with a plan of action in behalf of His autonomous Son, for mutual desired praise and glory.

Headship is evidenced by the inherent capacity of the Son to voluntarily yield to and concur with the leading of the Father for mutually desired purposes and glory.

Headship Of Man Defined

'Head' depicts a natural, voluntary, thoughtful compliance of the members of a body with the intents and desires of the head.[56]

For man, true headship is the inherent right of man to lead in a course of action that does not conflict with his Head, in behalf of woman for mutually desired praise. Headship is also evidenced by the inherent capacity of woman to voluntarily yield to and concur with the leading of man, without conflict, for mutually desired purposes and glory.

---

[56] In a different context Paul illustrates the head of the body of believers naturally directing the arms, feet, eyes, ears, etc. for the benefit of the whole body. The members of the body, both man and woman, respond willingly to the direction of the Head, who, in this analogy is Christ. (12:13,27)

The precept of headship illustrates a natural, thoughtful compliance of one mind with another.

Headship is an inherent principle that links authority and autonomy together.

Paul's brief statement on headship is not without context. Its principles and examples were relevant to his next admonition on head covering. By imposing their opinionated standard of outward appearance for worship, they had failed to honor the God-ordained precept of headship. The authority of biblical headship must facilitate autonomy. There must be a leading and a following. Rather, the Corinthians were striving with one another about what the correct head covering custom should be, which is why he informed them about headship.

6 The Woman's Rights

The biblical teaching of headship has no downside. Created in God's image, it is one of the essential, natural features for positive relation between man and woman. If, therefore, woman understands that headship is not synonymous with governance, she can avert sinful whims of man's irrational, religious authoritarianism.

Of course, after the Fall, faithful practice of man's status as head of woman became impossible. When the terms of headship are misunderstood, even believers default to an authoritarian stance over woman. Man's default to dictate rather than lead, to rebel rather than yield, makes woman vulnerable to error. It is at this point that she understands the biblical principles and functions of real headship for her spiritual wellbeing. Since the only antidote for domination and abuse is the Scripture, to practice this precept, woman must have the liberty to know and understand scripture for herself. The Bible alone provides needful instruction and examples for women.

WOMAN'S AUTONOMY FOR MARRIAGE

Abraham describes the qualifications for the wife of his son Isaac to his servant. Under an oath, this servant committed himself to accompany Isaac to find a wife for Isaac from Abraham's relatives, not the Canaanites. (Gen. 24:1-9, 57) Rebekah had gained her brother's and mother's approval, but she was not commanded to go with Abraham's servant and Isaac. This should serve as an example of man's headship. As head of the household, Laban honored his sister's wishes in this matter. Rebekah was not coerced; she followed voluntarily, having the right to refuse to go with Isaac.

WOMAN'S AUTONOMY IN OWNERSHIP

Under the banner of religion, the Pharisees devoured the houses of widows. Jesus drew one such example to the disciples' attention. A woman had thrown her last two coins into the temple treasury, representing her entire livelihood. Jesus explained to His disciples that the Pharisees had given out of their abundance, but she out of her poverty. (Matt. 23:24; Mk. 12:38-44)

It is assumed that Jesus complimented the woman. But, Jesus just stated the facts. The Pharisees were rich; the woman was poor. Having given everything, the woman gave disproportionately more than the Pharisees. Under the OT administration, she was only required to give a tithe, not everything. Misled, this woman was unable to discern how she was being robbed, consequently, she actually failed to give according to the Law. Instead of headship leadership, ungodly religionists robbed a vulnerable woman. Rather than honoring the precept of headship, these religious Pharisees ignored the Scriptures they claimed to know, "A good man leaves an inheritance to his children's children." (Prov. 13:22a) They were religious thieves.

Paul echoes this instruction when he says that children ought not to save for the parents, but parents for the children. (2 Cor.12:14) God does not expect women to subject themselves to church male authority in regards to money, yet churches still continues to prey on the poor.

Our Lord never commanded anyone to give everything he owns. Christ certainly required that those who followed Him take up his cross and follow Him. (Matt. 16:24,25) But denying oneself does not have anything to do with being poor. It has to do with not spending one's wealth on self-indulgent sinful pleasures. How can one follow Christ, if he gives all his wealth away and has nothing with which to buy food and clothing?

Man, and unfortunately the church, has drawn women into giving away their money for the 'Lord's work'. These Pharisaical <u>men</u> abused their position as head of woman and took advantage of them. This poor woman had no obligation to comply with the religious governance of men who did not recognize Christ as their Head.

WOMAN'S AUTONOMY IN FELLOWSHIP

The Apostle John alerted the elect lady to false teachers who taught that Christ had not really come in the flesh. Having the right to deny these men entry, she must have owned her home. It is interesting that John expects this woman to be discerning about the truth. Without any necessity to appeal to another man as 'head', this woman had the right and authority in her own household to deny entry to men who were false teachers. (2 John 10)

Jewish women were participants in the synagogue assembly. Not only did they attend the services, there was no division between men and women in the first century. Also, women qualified as part of the quorum

The Woman's Rights

of ten required to form a synagogue congregation, but were not allowed to read the Scriptures publicly. The synagogue system of instruction was rabbinical – question and answer. Paul discouraged women to ask questions.[57] (1 Cor. 14:34, 35)

WOMAN'S AUTONOMY IN PUBLIC SERVICE

Deborah stands out as an example of how God used a woman while men had failed to lead Israel. Identified as a prophetess, she gained a reputation for wisdom. Many in Israel came to seek her counsel. Rather than acquire authority over man, she deferred to Barak's leadership to defeat Israel's enemies. With the words, 'Has not the Lord gone before you?', she wants Barak to trust God for the victory. (Jud. 4:6, 14)

Deborah exemplifies the personal autonomy that belongs to every woman, yet appropriately submits to man's headship. She was not interested in personal governance or glory.

WOMAN'S AUTONOMY IN THE HOUSEHOLD

Paul desires younger women to marry, have children and <u>manage</u> their households. (1 Tim. 5:14) She is not instructed to ask her husband if she can manage her household. Married women manage household affairs while submitting to their own husbands so that the word of God is not held in disrepute. (Titus 2:5) Paul recognizes the woman's autonomy.

WOMAN'S AUTONOMY IN PERSONAL UNDERTAKINGS

The Bible has many examples of autonomous, enterprising women.

Naomi decided to return to her homeland without asking any man. Her Gentile daughter-in-law, Ruth, insisted on accompanying Naomi in the difficult journey back from Moab to Israel, after the loss of their husbands.

An excellent wife is also described as a businesswoman. Others praise her for being a woman of means. She buys and sells to make a profit to plant a vineyard. She does it for her husband, not because he commanded her to, but because she fulfilled the role God had given her as a woman. She also does it for her children, of course, who along with her husband, call her blessed! But most of all, this woman is to be praised, because she fears the Lord. (Prov.31:10-31) She recognizes God as her ultimate authority and as a woman filled her God-ordained role.

---

[57] Shmuel Safrai, *The Place of Women in First-Century Synagogues*, 2002 Priscilla Papers p. 9-11 https://www.cbeinternational.org/sites/default/files/pp161_3tpowifcs_0.pdf

Lydia was a seller of purple fabrics. (Ac. 16:14-15) The Lord opened her heart to receive the gospel. She received the gospel message, because the Lord opened her heart, not the authority of man.

WOMAN'S AUTONOMY IN WORSHIP

Was the woman who washed Jesus' feet lewd and inappropriate? (Matt. 26:6-10; Jn. 12:3) Not according to Jesus! He praised her for her devotion and her worship.

WOMAN'S RIGHT TO MAN'S HEAD

It is vital that believers appreciate that the term 'head' in no way enslaves the woman to man's authority. Understood from the biblical context, headship is actually a protection against man's abuse.

The woman's defense against overbearing or domineering governance is her knowledge of the fact that Christ is the Head of man, whether he recognizes it or not. Woman is to defer to man's influence and leading in the assembly of believers, but she is not obligated to obey arbitrary religious ritual that cannot be supported from Scripture.

WOMAN'S RIGHT TO TRUTH

Given man's failure in communicating truth, what recourse does the woman have? Knowing that Christ, as the Head, never failed in communicating His will to man, she must also have the means by which she can verify what man has told her the will of Christ is. Except for principles of moderation, no scripture even implies that woman must be instructed how to dress for worship. Woman may appeal to Scripture.

WOMAN'S RIGHT TO EXERCISE HER CREATED ROLE

Given the different customs and styles of dress, woman is free to continue to dress according to her custom. Far too often man has claimed authority with opinion that supersedes the Scriptures. (4:6) Designated as head of woman precludes any claim to be king of woman.

Marital Abuse

Many years ago, I knew a young professing Christian couple planning to be married. After their marriage, however, it became evident that all was not well. He had begun to discourage her from associating with her family. Despite having her own source of income, he controlled her shopping habits. When her clothing became tattered, she was commanded to mend them, while he indulged himself with things that he wanted. She dutifully packed a lunch when they went out shopping together. Clearly,

The Woman's Rights

he had interfered with the woman's role as a helper, in this case his wife. He had no understanding of biblical headship.

Cases like this are evidence of a total misunderstanding of Paul's actual marital teaching in Eph. 5:22-24, where it is wrongly supposed that to be subject to her husband "in everything" precludes exceptions. Note that Paul's exhortation is qualified. Wives are to submit to their own husbands, as to the Lord. To know how to submit to the Lord, wives must be knowledgeable. The church has a perfect Head; the wife does not. Secondly, the verb 'subject' is in the middle voice, indicating that the wife subjects herself to her husband's wishes. She is autonomous, therefore not obligated to obey everything her husband tells her. The wife is exhorted to submit to her husband as it is fit in the Lord. (Col. 3:18) The phrase, 'as unto the Lord' has the same import. She is to be discerning and yield to her own husband's wishes only when he does not violate biblical principles. The wife is exhorted to submit to her husband in everything as the church is exhorted to submit to Christ. Submission is therefore conditional. (Acts 5:29)

Headship never interferes with God-given roles.

WOMAN'S EXAMPLE IS MAN'S HEAD

How is the woman able to challenge the authority or leadership of man when she discerns it to be wrong? Immediately before Paul began talking about headship, he said, "Imitate me, just I also imitate Christ". (11:1 NKJV) To evaluate man's influence and authority, she can appeal to Paul's own words, written to woman as well as man, 'Follow me as I follow Christ'. Thus governance of woman is thwarted. As a man, Paul recognized that his authority was valid only as he followed Christ.

Christ's headship of man is always in accordance with the Father's will. On the other hand, depraved man ignores his Head, deferring to his own will. So, Paul informs these divisive Corinthians that man is not his own head, Christ is. And, his inability to submit to his perfect Head prevents him from being a perfect head of woman. Yet, the terms of headship cannot be different for man as they are for God. Though man's headship has not been abrogated, his authority is qualified.

Because it was impossible for the Father to exercise unreasonable and unrighteous authority and because it was impossible for the Son to follow unreasonable and unrighteous authority, they serve as the only perfect example of the doctrine of headship. Woman is not expected to follow man's lead if the matter in question dishonors the headship of Christ. (11:1) Man's headship is directly linked to the will of another – Christ. Again, Paul said, 'Follow me as I follow Christ.' (11:1)

SUMMARY

These are just a few biblical examples that show how woman is accorded the right to her own autonomy within her God-given role.

- Woman does not need man's permission to exercise her God-given role, i.e. managing their own household.
- Woman is not inferior to man.
- Woman has authority over her personal property.
- Woman has authority over her own business enterprise.
- Woman's role compliments man's role.
- Woman can discern false teachings for herself.
- Woman can deny entry of false teachers into her house.
- Woman has the right to know everything the man knows about following Christ. (11:1)

To rightly understand Paul's precept of headship, we must not lose sight of his preceding exhortation to follow him as he follows Christ. Headship implies that someone is following.

After the Fall, the relation between man and woman defaulted from headship to governance of man over woman. Given the propensity of man to govern, Paul informs them of the headship precept, which is antithetical to governance.

Exemplary women in Scripture show no desire to have authority over man. Neither did godly men engage in a quest to dominate women. Had the Corinthian believers practiced the headship <u>precept</u>, the woman's headship <u>dilemma</u> would also have vanished.

7 The Expected Admonition

The overwhelming opinion is that Paul censured men for praying with head covered and women for praying with head uncovered. But is this consistent with what we know of Paul?

The preceding summaries of OT head wear, the traditions actually delivered to the church, prevailing head wear customs in Corinth, and the precept of headship should help us understand how Paul might rule or not rule on the head covering strife. But, let's look at the Apostle Paul in greater detail, in order to evaluate what admonition we might expect or might not expect from him on head covering.

Apostolic Authority

Paul's letter to the Corinthians is authoritative. Though self-described as 'least of the Apostles', he did not hesitate to exercise his God-given authority. (14:37; 15:9) But, would we expect Paul to make a unilateral apostolic regulations for worship head covering?

Apostolic Authority Is Appointed

After the Lord ascended, the Apostles recognized that they were given the Lord's commandments through the Holy Spirit. (Ac. 1:2) Paul testified that he was called by the Lord to be an Apostle. (Rom.1:1; Ga. 1:1) He understood that the source of truth was not human. (Eph. 3:5) Paul's declared that his words are the 'commandments of the Lord'. (14:37) Like the Prophets, the Apostles were the Lord's spokesmen.

Apostolic Authority Is United

After Christ ascended, believers recognized the Apostles. (Ac. 2:37) Before Paul was converted, the other eleven Apostles agreed with Peter that they ought to obey God rather than men. (Ac. 5:29) Later, as part of Council of Jerusalem, they, together with the elders arrived at a consensus on the Jewish religious custom of circumcision. (Ac. 15:19-29)

Apostolic Authority Is Leadership

The impulse to govern others, rather than lead, is also evident among believers. Two disciples vied for their own throne when Jesus would establish His kingdom. But Jesus told His disciples that 'it shall not be so among you.' (Matt. 20:25, 26) Paul did not say, 'Be governed by me, as I am governed by Christ.' However, with authority Paul could say, "Be ye followers of me, even as I also am of Christ." (1 Cor. 11:1; KJV) A governor is not required to do what he commands others to do. A leader does. This is the background context for Paul's teaching on the headship of Christ. Paul understood that his authority was not governance, but leadership. Governors don't lead.

APOSTOLIC AUTHORITY DECLARES TRUTH

Paul recognized that the Lord had given the apostles authority for the purpose of edification. (2 Cor. 10:8) Among other things, Paul commended himself to believers 'by the word of truth.' Despite persecutions for preaching the truth, he could not be distracted from the truth. (2 Cor. 6:7; 7:14; 11:10; 13:8)

His authoritative advice to the churches of Galatia, Colossae and Corinth was not arbitrary, unique or new. His exhortations were commensurate with the Scriptures and the other Apostles. Paul considered himself no less than the chief of apostles. (2 Cor. 11:5; 12:11)

APOSTOLIC AUTHORITY FACILITATES UNITY

The Corinthians kept the ordinance of baptism, yet pridefully valued status based on who baptized them. They kept the Lord's Table, yet participated in these meals selfishly. If uniformity of these ordained traditions did not prevent their sinful divisions, how would a ruling to comply with single head covering be any different? Had Paul legislated a uniform rule for head covering and hair length for worship, the Corinthians would have yet another excuse to judge one another.

APOSTOLIC AUTHORITY IS OBJECTIVE

Paul scolded Peter publicly for his inconsistent fellowship with Jews and Gentiles. (Ga. 2:11-15) Apostolic authority was not a respecter of persons, in dealing with sin.

SUMMARY

As an Apostle, he was a leader, a promoter of unity in the truth of the Gospel, willing to expose sin. How could different head covering customs be sin and contrary to the truth of His word? These defining features of apostolic authority raises serious doubts regarding the notion that Paul had instituted worship wear regulations.

PAUL'S TEACHING

From what is known of Paul's knowledge and teaching, would we expect him to solve the Corinthian conflict by stipulating the worshipers' outward appearance? Or, would he be addressing their attitudes?

PAUL'S MORAL EXHORTATIONS ARE ABSOLUTE

Morality was never in any doubt. Theft, covetousness, fornication, etc. are always sinful. (6:9,10) If we were to expect Paul to censure a custom, it would have clear moral implications. He does not explain how head covering customs could have moral implications.

PAUL AFFIRMED THE 'DELIVERED' TRADITIONS

Paul did not rule on traditions absolutely, except those that were 'delivered' to him from the Lord. Baptism and the Lord's Table outwardly depicted the inward reality of the Gospel in the life of the believer and for that reason were special. He had commended them for keeping these ordinances, but admonished them for <u>how</u> they were keeping them.

PAUL TAUGHT THAT TRADITIONS WERE OPTIONAL

Paul was not opposed to observing various customs.

Former Traditions Were Not To Be Imposed

Paul excoriated the Galatian churches for preaching another gospel when they compelled professing believers to be circumcised. (Gal.1:7-9, 14; 2:3) He exhorted the Colossian church not to be subject to religious observances because they only serve to accentuate the fleshly appetite with a false humility. (Col. 2:16-21) Having stated that circumcision profits nothing, to then introduce head covering protocol, would just be switching from one legalistic track to another.

Former Traditions Were Not Censured

Evidently, both Jew and Gentile Corinthians were clinging to their respective ethnic and religious customs in public worship gatherings. Since Paul was not concerned about his outward appearance when he allowed his hair to grow according to the Nazarite vow, it is inconceivable that he would make up a rule that would not apply to him. (11:14,15) Paul did not prohibit Jewish traditions such as the Nazarite vow or circumcision for Jews.

In order not to be a distraction to their gospel ministry to Jews, Paul circumcised Timothy, a Jew. Believers could still be unified as they continued to practice traditions of their choice.

Traditions Must Not Offend A Weaker Believer.

More informed believers had offended recent converts from pagan idolatry by eating meat that had been offered to idols. Though this offered-to-idols meat would not cause personal spiritual injury to the seasoned believer, a new believer, with recent memories of his idolatry, might be unduly diverted from his fellowship with other believers and God. In this case, believers were advised not to eat this meat. Unconverted idolaters might also perceive believers, who ate this dedicated meat, to be compromising their faith and testimony. (8:1-13; 10:27-30)

PAUL TAUGHT THEM TO FELLOWSHIP IN THE GOSPEL

Weak or strong, Jew or Gentile, bond or free, all believers were to be equally accepted in the fellowship. Paul himself stated that both circumcision and uncircumcision are nothing. (7:19) He encouraged believers that whatever gift they had, they were not deficient. (1:7) But he admonished them for their sectarianism based on leadership. (1:10-17)

SUMMARY

Had there been only one offensive head covering tradition to converted Jews, Romans and Greeks alike, then, based on his counsel on eating sacrificed meat, Paul might have appealed to believers to comply with one custom for conscience sake. But, since the Romans, Greeks and Jewish priests worshiped differently, the head covering quarrel raised the specter of competing options that could not be satisfied with one mandate, as with meat that had been offered to idols. On the one hand, the Roman would be offended when a Greek would worship with his head uncovered according to his tradition. On the other hand, the Greek would be offended by the Roman who worshiped with his head covered according to his tradition. Now, whose conscience would set the standard?

If inappropriate head covering were truly a sin, there is no doubt that Paul would have expressly forbidden it. Knowing Paul's treatment of Jewish ritual, it is impossible to explain why Paul would replace diversity with uniformity, which would exacerbate the division.

SCRIPTURAL AUTHORITY

Another means of knowing what to expect from an exhortation on head coverings is Paul's knowledge and regard for Scripture. We would expect Paul not to contradict himself.

The Expected Admonition

PAUL REFERENCED SCRIPTURE

Paul had excelled in his study as a Pharisee. In 1 Corinthians alone he quotes from the OT 18 times and alludes to it 23 times.[58] Familiar with the OT, Paul draws upon the OT often to emphasize his point. His exhortations and warnings to flee idolatry and unbelief are accompanied by inspired commentary from Israel's wilderness wanderings. (10:1-12) Had there been an expected protocol for believers in worship, he would have referenced the OT, as he did on other matters. Paul even references the Genesis account of creation to show the origin of headship, but not a single reference to an OT practice of head covering.

PAUL AFFIRMED THE BEREAN'S RIGHT TO VERIFY WITH SCRIPTURE

Again, it is particularly noteworthy that the Bereans verified Paul's message with Scripture before accepting it, and were complimented for being noble. (Ac.17:10,11) Paul did <u>not</u> exhort them by saying, 'You no longer have to deal with the OT scriptures because the things I, as an Apostle of Christ, am now telling you are new and not found in the OT.' Neither did they say, 'Let us check this out with the 'pastor' or a rabbi.' The Corinthians also had the same right to appeal to the OT.

PAUL ALSO COULD NOT EXCEED WHAT WAS WRITTEN

As an antidote to human wisdom, he exhorted the Corinthian church not to exceed what has been written. (3:19-23; 4:6) Certain leaders were favored by their own 'wisdom', rather than the wisdom of God found in OT Scripture. (see 3:19) Unwarranted appreciation for ability gifts was based on their own 'wisdom'.

Given the total silence of Scripture on the matter of head covering, what do we suppose Paul would do? (4:6) One commentator writes,

> "Revere the *silence* of Holy Writ, as much as its *declarations*;' so you will less dogmatize on what is not expressly revealed (Deut.29:29)."[59]

Paul's appreciation and use of the OT Scripture as authority to support his teaching is evidence that he understood that his apostleship did not license him to alter Scripture, so legislation on head covering and hair length would not be expected.

---

[58] Blue Letter Bible Study Resources, All of Paul's letters contain numerous quotations from the OT and allusions to the OT.
[59] Jamieson Fausset and Brown, *Commentary on The Whole Bible*, P.1195

Circumcision Was Not A Unilateral Apostolic Directive

It is noteworthy that the tradition of circumcision was commanded to Moses, yet not expected of the Gentile Jethro, Moses' father-in-law, who also worshiped God. Neither is there any record that when Nebuchadnezzar recognized God and worshiped Him that he was circumcised. Paul knew that not every believer had to be part of the nation of Israel and he also knew that not everyone who was circumcised truly worshipped God. (10:5-8) Circumcision and other religious rituals served as types and symbols to foreshadow the Person and work of Christ in the New Covenant. Paul himself continued with Jewish tradition to win the Jews, but new converts were not expected to observe these religious rituals.

SUMMARY

Paul's consistent approach to dealing with conflicts helps us to know what to expect from the Apostle in solving the issue of head covering. Having to scold the church for the manner in which they were keeping the Lord's required traditions of Baptism and the Lord's Table, it is untenable that he would require a new tradition that wasn't delivered by the Lord. That this Apostle would introduce a custom, by which one might gage his worship, is obviously incompatible with his apostolic authority, teaching and example. Paul was determined to give no reason for offense either to the Jews or Greeks. (10:31-33) He would not be expected to rule on outward uniformity, but rather inward unity. To regulate head coverings for worship would be yet another potential for conflict. So, given Paul's own teaching, his traditions, his apostleship and regard for the OT scriptures, it would be surprising for us to find that Paul ever demanded head covering protocol and/or hair length for worship.

Yet, these expectations notwithstanding, many commentators believe that Paul did in fact regulate head coverings during prophesying and praying. The task remaining, then, is to examine the single passage in all of Scripture, used to claim that he did. (11:4-16) Is it possible that Paul's teaching on head coverings has been misread?

8 Praying and Prophesying

The customs that concerned Paul pertained to the time of prayer and prophesying. Some had expected head covering etiquette during 'worship'. (11:4,5) Professing believers were prone then, as they still are today, to commend themselves to God with contrived rituals.

A little background about how the services of Paul's day were conducted, will assist our understanding of what is meant by 'praying and prophesying'.

THE APOSTOLIC SERVICE

The consensus among commentators is that the Christian assembly was based on the synagogue service. Since the first converts were mostly Jewish, it was natural to carry on with the format they had been accustomed to, but with adjustments to accommodate the worship of Christ and the NT writings. Following is a summary of content and probable order of the Corinthian service, gleaned from several sources, including a Bible Dictionary[60] and 1 Corinthians 14,

- Recitation of the Shema. This is a confession of faith from De. 6:4-9; 11:13-21; Nu. 15:37-41. This is a biblical prayer.
- Praying the Shemoneh Esreh. (Tefillah)[61] The ruler of the synagogue selected the person to pray this prayer, each sabbath. The congregation would make specific responses, especially the 'amen' at the end of each blessing. This was a rabbinical prayer rather than biblical.[62]
- Reading of the Torah Scripture, not translations. At least three verses were read, not recited.
- The reading was translated into the vernacular.

---

[60] Merrill F. Unger, *Unger's Bible Dictionary*, Synagogue, p, 1054

[61] Shemoneh Esrei, *Reciting the weekly Amidah prayers*. This was the chief prayer, which every Israelite was taught to repeat, at least in part, three times a day. This prayer was composed in the fifth century B.C.E., by 120 men of the Great Assembly.
https://www.hebrew4christians.com

[62] Bible Encyclopedias, *1901 Jewish Encyclopedia*, Liturgy
https://www.studylight.org/encyclopedias/eng/tje/l/liturgy.html

- A paragraph was read from the Prophets in the Scripture, not translations. The reader could choose the selection. (Lk. 4:17)
- The reading of the Prophets was translated into the vernacular.
- The Scriptures read were then explained by a maximum of three members of the congregation. (Cor. 14:29)
- The lecture was translated into the vernacular, if necessary. (1 Cor. 14:13, 27,28)
- Antiphonal chanting of a poem, likely from the Psalms. (1 Cor. 14:26)[63]
- The service closed with a blessing to which everyone says, 'Amen'. (1 Cor. 14:16)

Near the end of the service, the leader might read new correspondence from the Apostles. The Lord's Supper was probably a weekly occurrence. The primary parts of the service pertain to prayer and instruction.

THE LANGUAGE DISTRACTION

Due to the multilingual composite of the congregation, participants wanted to teach in his own native language. Those lacking proficiency in the vernacular, were permitted to speak their own language, if interpreters were available. But Paul limits the number of speakers to three in order to allow time for the translation of each into the vernacular, which everyone understood. The services would have been unbearable had one language been translated into all the minority languages.

Though multilingual, everyone could not speak the Greek vernacular well enough to be understood, so Paul had instructed the church to allow men of different languages speak, if a translator was present. If they could not speak the Greek well enough, they were to remain silent. So, all public discourse was to be translated into the Greek vernacular.

THE REVELATION DISTRACTION

Errant inferences from 'praying and prophesying', have characterized the Corinthians as inspired by God. Both continuationists and cessationists teach that believers were personally gifted by the Holy Spirit to reveal new truth.[64] Had these men and women been receiving new

---

[63] Dr. D.W. Ekstrand, *Worship In The Early Church*, http://www.thetransformedsoul.com/additional-studies/

[64] Robert L. Thomas, *Understanding Spiritual Gifts*, p.60. Cessationism teaches that the supposed supernatural gifts ceased in the apostolic era. Continuationism teaches that some of the supernatural gifts continue to the present day.

Praying and Prophesying

revelation from the Lord, then, why was it even necessary for Paul to write them? Why did the Holy Spirit not reveal much needed 'new revelation' in Paul's letter? The view that the 'gift of prophecy' was an ability given to these careless Corinthians to prophesy 'new truth' is groundless.

Who then were the Corinthian 'prophets'?

THE 'PROPHET' SPEAKERS

Paul calls these speakers, 'prophets'. Essentially, a 'prophet' is a forth-teller. The Corinthian 'prophets' were not inspired to reveal truth, as were God's appointed primary Prophets and Apostles. (14:37)

An example of a 'secondary' prophet was Aaron. Designated by God to be Moses' prophet, everything God spoke to Moses, Aaron would speak to Pharaoh. (Ex.7:1,2) Similarly, the prophets in Corinth would 'speak forth' to explain what was already written in the OT in addition to what the Apostles had written.

Under the false assumption that the basic function of a 'prophet' is to predict, it is believed that men and women were overwhelmed with some new personally revealed truth directly from God. However, Paul informed believers that 'prophets', who <u>thought</u> they received 'revelations' directly from the Lord, were actually not the commandments of the Lord. (14:36,37) The Corinthian 'prophets' were not inspired!

If God had truly revealed new truth to these 'prophets', it would not be necessary for the message of the 'speaking prophet' to be judged. (14:29,30) The Corinthian 'prophet' was a speaking minister who endeavored to teach what had already been revealed through the Prophets and Apostles.

THE WOMAN'S SILENCE

Since it is clear that Paul was not against women praying and prophesying in assembly, there must have been other reasons for Paul's censure of women. (11:4,5; 14:34) Women were not segregated in the first century synagogue assemblies. [65]

The First Class Conditional[66]

At first glance, it appears that Paul implied that women mostly did not want to learn. (1 Cor. 14:35) But that is not the case. By using the 'first

---

[65] Shmuel Safrai, *The Place of Women In First Century Synagogues*, p. 10
https://www.cbeinternational.org/sites/default/files/pp161_3tpowifcs_0.pdf

[66] Greek Conditional Sentences in the New Testament. (Rom. 6:5 is similar)
http://www.ntgreek.org/pdf/conditional_sentences.pdf

class condition', Paul, for the sake of argument, presumes true that these women did indeed want to learn! Firstly, they showed up at the meeting. Secondly, they attempted to ask questions in their own language to gain understanding. Presuming their genuine desire to learn, he provides his solution, that is, to ask the men (*andras*) of their own households when they got home because doctrinal matters were discussed among men. Fourthly, there is no indication that the women wanted to be teachers. They wanted to ask questions.

The Woman's Silence is Specific

The 'sermon' followed the reading of Scripture. However, in the first century synagogues, the sermon was more like a lesson where the teacher invited questions from his listeners. This was the customary rabbinical question and answer manner of teaching.[67] Similarly, in the NT church, a 'prophet' spoke, then the rest would judge. (14:29) The context of the woman's silence pertains to asking questions in a meeting of both men and women. (14:34, 35)

PROPHESYING AS A CONGREGATION

As stated above, the verb, 'prophesy' means to 'tell forth'. (Vine's) The work of 'prophesy' is not restricted to an ordained 'prophet' or 'apostle'. The OT provides further context and example for our understanding of the prophesying Corinthians.

Israel Congregational Participation

Both men and women had gathered together at the Water Gate where they asked Ezra to bring forth the Law. After Ezra read the Law, he pronounced the blessing upon them and they answered with an "Amen". (Neh. 8:1-11)

Corinthian Congregational Participation

Jews and Gentiles orally participated together as a congregation. Among the Jews, the Hebrew Scriptures were still read and memorized. To what extent men and women would recite prayer, scripture and song together history is unclear, but Paul expected that everyone understood the prayers in order to say 'Amen'. (14:16)

---

[67] Shmuel Safrai, *The Place of Women In First Century Synagogues*, p. 11
https://www.cbeinternational.org/sites/default/files/pp161_3tpowifcs_0.pdf

Praying and Prophesying

THE VERBS ARE PASSIVE

'Praying' and 'prophesying' are in the passive voice. (11:4, 5) This means that the subject is being acted upon by another influence. Of course, this raises the question of how one could pray or prophesy passively. What, indeed, is that influence? Most commentators believe that the Holy Spirit was revealing new truth to both men and women. In the exercise of this supposed gift, women were to be covered. But as already discussed, women were instructed not to ask questions of the speaking ministers. Why, then, the passive voice?

Praying and Prophesying Passively

Neither the text nor context allow for the notion that individuals were mystically receiving revelation from the Holy Spirit, causing them to speak unlearned languages. Congregants would recite the Shema, which contained both prophetic (prescriptive) truth and prayers and songs from scripture. Scripture, especially the Psalms, would be chanted or sung. In prayer, like today, the leader would offer a prayer to which the listener would give his assent. So, with the passive, the grammar indicates that congregants, who prayed and prophesied, did not initiate the content. Recitation of prophecies and prayers from Scripture was passive, because it was in response to the leader. Joining in prayer, chanting the Psalms or reciting from the Law, is to prophesy Scripture or pray passively.

SUMMARY

It is noteworthy that in the OT dispensation, men from all eleven tribes and most of the tribe of Levi were barred from religious service. Only Aaron's descendants were delegated to be the priests to serve in the temple and teach the people. (Mal. 2:7) All other men were excluded from the teaching ministry.

Given the multiple languages spoken, Paul determined that women should refrain from asking questions during the rabbinical style of teaching used in the synagogues and early churches. So, Paul counseled the women not to interrupt the speaking prophet, but rather to ask the men of their acquaintance at home. (14:34) It is in this sense that Paul instructed Timothy that women ought to remain silent in the church. (1 Tim. 2:11-15) Since most churches today do not have a question and answer time, Paul's instruction would not be applicable. However, the context and grammar indicate, that in chorus, both men and women were praying and prophesying together.

Imagined Context

Some think that the customs of headdress applied only to individuals, man or woman, who prayed or prophesied publicly. Man's head must be uncovered; woman's head must be covered. Thus, man and woman were qualified to speak to the congregation as revelation prophets and prophetesses. But the text neither states nor implies that women were entitled to preach sermons if they wore head coverings. And, neither man nor woman was revealing new truth from the Lord.

Therefore, 'praying and prophesying' can only refer to the corporate participation of both man and woman in the services. The context is clear that women were orally praying and prophesying together as a chorus with the men. Together men and women recited prayers and said 'amen' to a prayer, and prophesied by forth telling truth memorized from the Shema and other portions of scripture. (Psa.106:48)

'Praying and Prophesying' Today

Not that long ago it was common for the congregation to read portions of scripture responsively or recite what is known as 'The Lord's Prayer'. The Psalms, many of them prayers, and other passages of praise and doctrine were read in unison by the entire congregation. Like then, men and women today have also been prophesying and praying together as they did in the synagogues and apostolic churches.

It is therefore untenable that believers in the Corinthian church had the gift of revelation that would enable them to prophesy new truth. Yet, this erroneous teaching continues to draw professing believers to search for 'prophetic' truth where it does not exist.

9 The Actual Coverings

Among other Corinthian delinquencies reviewed in the first chapter, the church had allowed different head covering customs to cause further division. Without any biblical or historical evidence, it is assumed by many commentators that the verb 'dishonors' implies a precept for an expected head covering custom.

COMMENTARY ASSUMPTIONS

The following highlights incidents where otherwise sound commentators have made assumptions that overlook both the grammar and context of Paul's lesson on head covering.

ASSUMPTION: HEAD COVERING SHOWS WOMAN'S 'SUBJUGATION'

Albert Barnes notes that a head covering was the traditional mark of the sex and her subordination.[68] A man wearing a veil or turban was a "mark of servitude or inferiority," thus inserting the master/servant idea into the text. But Paul is only exhorting them about the time spent in prayer and prophesying, saying nothing about a supposed necessity to wear something on their heads after the worship service.

ASSUMPTION: HEAD COVERING DEPICTS HEADSHIP

Commentators all ignore the actual features of headship, none of which have to do with outward appearance. By drawing attention to their practice of 'dishonoring', Paul implicates the church for failing to appreciate the meaning of headship. Headship is about essential functions, not superior status. Omitting the headship doctrine from the head covering issue, jeopardizes a correct understanding of Paul's exhortation. Where man has failed to follow the perfect leading of Christ, woman has the option to reject the imperfect leading of man.

A Missing Link Of Logic

Both man and woman have a 'head', yet, commentators provide no reason why man's headship is depicted by a woman covering her head and

---

[68] *Albert Barnes Notes on The Whole Bible*, Please see verses 5 and 7
https://www.studylight.org/commentaries/bnb/1-corinthians-11.html

why Christ's headship is not depicted with man's covered head. Furthermore, woman is expected to cover in the presence of an imperfect head, yet man is not expected to cover in the worship of the perfect Head.

If head covering was required to depict headship, Paul would have given an example where Christ prayed covered. Really, if covering during prayer and prophesying is required on the basis of headship, then both Christ and man also need head covering.

ASSUMPTION: WORSHIP HEAD COVERING IS GENDER SPECIFIC

Paul referred to man's head apparel as 'something hanging down' indicating that a hoody type garment or shawl may have been used during worship. (11:4) Woman, on the other hand, would have worn a covering tied up in typical woman's fashion. Both man or woman could be wearing something on the head in a style appropriate for their gender. We know that in that day both men and women wore dresses. But the design of the garment and how it was worn, were unique to the sex.

The notion that Paul was regulating headwear to minimize sexual confusion for the heavenly beings is baseless. (chapter 16) They ignore the fact that OT regulation had already prescribed different fabric and style for male and female apparel. Sexual identity and confusion was not the subject of Paul's admonition. Had some men been wearing feminine scarves, and conversely, if the women had been wearing masculine styles, he would have admonished them accordingly.

SUMMARY

Various head covering views notwithstanding, it is sufficient to state that commentators have all rightly discerned that there was an issue with which God was not pleased. But what was it - actually?

Commentators have assumed that a different head covering precept for each gender. Most infer from this passage that head covering signaled woman's subjugation to man, that woman must be dressed for the angels, that headship implies unilateral authority. These are just some of the unbiblical commentary perspectives, if left unanswered, leave the church exposed to just another legalistic trend. For this reason, the supposition that Paul had censured the Corinthians for not complying with head covering protocol during prayer and prophesying, is central to this debate. If Paul was not concerned about head covering during prayer and prophesying, what was his solution to the strife over this matter?

The Actual Coverings

THE SCRIPTURAL FACTS

Paul states a fact that man and woman dishonor their head by not heeding accepted custom.

> 4) Every man praying or prophesying having anything down from his head, dishonors the head of him.
>
> 5) Moreover, every woman praying or prophesying with her head uncovered dishonors the head of her; indeed it is one and the same with having been shaven.[69]

Paul first addresses head covering as it pertains to men. (11:4) There is much debate what is meant by 'down from his head' in verse 4. Some teach that this is a reference to letting hair 'hang down'.[70] Others say this was part of the man's garment that would be pulled over his head while in prayer, thus hanging from his head. And others think that this pertains to the prayer shawl of the Jews, the tallit.

As the tradition pertains to women, most scholars think the problem centered on her not wearing a head covering. (11:5, 6) Others teach that Paul is referring to the woman's hair as her covering. (11:15) But this view fails to account for the fact that Paul gave the woman with a shaved head an option to don a head covering, which could not be anything but fabric. (11:6) For a woman to lack a head covering was to identify with those whose heads were shaved. (11:5)

HAIR FOR A COVERING

A few commentators argue that cloth covering has been imported into the text, that Paul was simply addressing the matter of hairstyles.[71] (11:3-7) For example, translating "with head covered" as 'having something down from his head', it is argued that this refers to hair exclusively. This argument fails in a couple of ways.

- If Paul had meant only 'hair hanging down', he could easily have used the Greek word for 'hair' as he did in verse 15.

---

[69] Interlinear Bible, biblehub.com

[70] *Coffman's Commentaries on the Bible*, on 1Cor.11:4

[71] *Coffman's Commentary of the Bible*. He states that translation has inhibited a right understanding of this passage. He states that vs. 4 should be 'something hanging down', which to him could only mean 'hair'. He maintains that the Greek translated 'uncovered' is simply a general word, meaning not completely covered, falling short of specifying a garment. (v.6) He concludes that a fabric head covering is imported into the text.

- Secondly, historical records depict men who wore head coverings as something that appeared to hang down.

The Greek for 'uncovered' implies the lack of a fabric head covering on the woman's head. (11:5) However, 'covered', meaning 'something hanging down', may not imply a cloth covering exclusively. (11:4) It could be that both hair and fabric were implied. But how could that be?

Paul's Long-Hair Experiences

Paul had shorn his hair according to a vow that he had made. According to the Nazarite vow, the hair was to be cut at the Temple in Jerusalem. Because Paul had his hair cut at Cenchrea, not at the Temple in Jerusalem, there is some debate as to whether he had made a Nazarite vow. (Acts 18:18-21) Though the duration of the vow is not known, it is reasonable to surmise that his hair would not be short at the time it was cut. Nonetheless, the context indicates that his vow compelled him to keep a feast in Jerusalem. Whether this cut was at the beginning of his vow or at the end, it was special. Near the end of the vow, his hair would be quite long.

Aquila and Priscilla Had A Hair Cut

Though not unanimous, some scholars contend that the Greek grammar in Acts 18:18 indicates that Aquila and Priscilla had also cut their hair in accordance with a vow. This might be one explanation why women in the congregation had shorn hair.

PREDOMINANT CLOTH COVERING CUSTOMS

Head covering customs spanned several cultures. As stated in chapter 4, it is believed that Greek men worshiped with their heads uncovered. Romans worshiped with their heads covered. The tallit was a later development but it is quite likely that converted Jewish priests continued to wear caps or turbans as prescribed for the maintenance and services of the temple. Had God intended a custom for everyone, not just the priests, He would have regulated head covering, as He did for the priesthood.

HEAD COVERING EXPECTATIONS

But who should relinquish their former customs? Jews, Greeks or Romans? If a Jewish man attended our service wearing a tallit or a skullcap (kippah), joined in the responsive reading of scripture, said 'Amen' to the prayer of the minister, sang along with the rest, would Paul say of him that

The Actual Coverings

he is dishonoring Christ? No. Yet, Paul clearly stated that the compliant were dishonoring their head of the non-compliant.

They had not recognized that Christ was the Head of <u>every</u> man, thus every man could not be the head of another. As Paul would teach in greater detail in the next chapter, Christ is the head of the body and He controls the movements of each member, Jew and Gentile, bond and free, man and woman. (12:27)

Had there been a previous OT head covering command for prayer and prophesying, Paul would have said so. And, since there is nothing in all of scripture that demanded man's head be uncovered and woman's head covered, during corporate worship, the notion that a head covering custom was required by Paul is unfounded.

Some men felt a religious obligation to pray with their heads covered as the Romans did. Jewish priests would likely also be inclined to cover, given the training they received in the service of the temple. The woman also had different customs. From Paul's text, some women, apparently a minority, did not feel the need to cover their head while praying and prophesying.

SUMMARY

Had hair length for man or woman been a hindrance to worship, Paul would certainly have censured Jews who carried on with this or any similar vow of consecration or purification. The common view that God was concerned with outward appearance during corporate worship conflicts with Paul's own practice. Since Paul himself took religious vows, he would not have prevented others from doing the same. (Acts 18:18)

With the Greek word meaning 'something hanging down', man was dishonored for having either long hair or a cloth covering during worship. (11:4) In short, man dishonored his head by having long hair or covering his head. Woman dishonored her head by having a shorn head or not covering her head.

The Corinthians had ignored OT history and contrived their own standard for worship. Does Paul's actual grammar show support the Corinthian head covering conflict?

10 The Actual Grammar

Paul states the facts of the Corinthian practice: a man having something hanging down from his head, and a woman having her head uncovered while praying or prophesying, dishonors the head. Had God approved this disgracing? After all, God intentionally 'shames' the wise and puts evil doers to shame. (1:27; 1 Pet.3:16). Or, was this an issue similar to the Corinthians 'shaming' of those who had nothing? (11:22)

Generally, it is assumed that those who 'dishonored' their head were the guilty party. God has a right to shame evil doers, but were those who violated a head covering protocol evil doers? Should those who failed to comply with a custom deserve shame? The grammar and context help us to understand who the inappropriate individuals were.

GRAMMAR AND MEANING

Again, our attention is devoted to verses 4 and 5, where the 'head' is dishonored during prayer and prophesying.

> [4] Every man praying or prophesying, having the head covered, doth dishonour his head,
>
> [5] and every woman praying or prophesying with the head uncovered, doth dishonour her own head, for it is one and the same thing with her being shaven, (11:4, 5; YLT)

Does the grammar and context teach that head covering customs for corporate prayer and prophesying are valid?

PRESENT INDICATIVE ACTIVE

The verb 'dishonors' means to shame or disgrace. Of 19 translations, 4 translate *kataischynei* as 'disgrace', 5 as 'shames' and 10 as 'dishonors'.

The verb 'dishonors' is 'present indicative active'. The indicative is a statement of fact, whether a precept or an existing practice. (11:4, 5) This means that the verb describes a current reality. This is not a command. It simply states that when man covered and woman did not cover during prayer, the compliant dishonored the non-compliant.

Paul used the same tense regarding headship in verse 3. His 'desiring' them to know doctrine actively, presently occupied his mind. He did not command them to make Christ the Head of man, and man the head of woman. He only wanted them to know the reality of this precept. Elsewhere, Paul uses this tense negatively, to say that circumcision or uncircumcision is nothing or avails nothing, without condemning either practice. (7:19; Ga. 5:6). This is a precept that anticipates either practice.

In our head covering text, Paul drew their attention to another active, present fact that pertained to 'dishonoring' behavior. It is obvious that the 'realities' of verses 4 and 5 were undesirable. But, who was responsible for the 'dishonor' some had been experiencing? Paul fully exposes the guilty party, as he speaks in the third person.

THE THIRD PERSON

Paul continues in the third person, writing about men and women who did not comply with expected customs for corporate worship. (11:4,5) It is important to note that he is not writing to men and women who did not comply with expected worship etiquette. His target audience was all the others who were not 'dishonoring' their heads. He is not exhorting anyone deemed inappropriate. Those who did not comply with the accepted custom did not dishonor anyone else, but themselves.

If Paul had wanted the non-compliant, who he is talking <u>about,</u> to stop violating this custom, why did he <u>not</u> speak <u>to</u> them directly in the second person as he did when He tells them to stop 'despising' and 'putting to shame' the needy at the Lord's Table? (11:22)

Paul does not state or imply that he wants these who are 'dishonoring' their own heads to stop their 'dishonoring' by complying with an artificial custom. Paul describes an existing reality. (11:4,5) As yet, there is no admonition for correction, no imperative.

'DISHONORS' IS NOT IN THE MIDDLE VOICE

The Greek construction also imputes responsibility to one party with the lack of the middle voice. The tense of the verb "dishonors" is present and in the active voice. (11:4, 5) Had this been written in the middle voice, the Corinthians would have understood that the man who covered his head not only initiated the action but also actively participated in the result of his action – dishonoring his head.[72] Therefore the non-compliant man or woman dishonors their head without participating in the action; they were not responsible for the result of their action.

---

[72] Please see *Greek Quick Reference Guide* at Precept Austin. Regarding the middle voice, "This voice means that the SUBJECT **initiates** the action and **participates** in the results of the action".

The Actual Grammar

SUMMARY

The word translated 'dishonors' or 'disgrace' by itself does not prove responsibility for an offense. But in the minds of the custom-keepers, the man who covered and the woman who did not, were guilty of a violation. When this letter was read to the church, it would be clear that this passage was not addressed to the man who covered and the woman who didn't. Since the verb 'dishonors' is in the third person and not in the middle voice, the shame showered upon the non-conformists originated from among those who complied with the custom. If the man who covered and the woman who didn't, were not to blame, for the dishonor incurred, then a head covering precept cannot be deduced from these verses.

FEATURES OF THE VIOLATION?

What were some of the features of this violation that caused so much conflict?

THE VIOLATION WAS RELIGIOUS

Because head-covering protocol was specific to the time of prayer and prophesying, it was a corporate religious expectation. This issue did not pertain to normal interactions at home and in the public. Different head covering practices during corporate worship led to judgmental assessments of one another.

THE VIOLATION WAS INADVERTENT

The non-compliant only dishonored their own head by wearing contrary head covering. But they bore no responsibility for the negative thoughts and opinions of the compliant who dishonored them. They had inadvertently dishonored themselves, by means of the malicious views of those who disagreed.

THE VIOLATION WAS COSMETIC

Since there had not been any Scriptural laws that demanded a standard head covering practice for worship, this custom was an opinion, apparently, held by the majority. The adjective 'shameful' gives us the sense of what is meant by the verb 'dishonor'. (11:6) For a woman to have her head uncovered was viewed as an embarrassment, like having her head shaved. One commentator elucidates on the origin of shame,

> "What Paul means to say then is: a woman praying with uncovered head stands in the eye of public opinion, guided as

it is by appearances, on just the same level with her who has the shorn hair of a courtesan."[73]

The 'shame' they endured came from the negative opinion and words of others about outward appearance.

THE VIOLATION DID NOT IMPLICATE PERSONAL GUILT

Non-conformity to a custom does not imply guilt. It bears repeating that since they had not complied with a uniform standard for head covering, this could not possibly have been a 'tradition' to which they were 'holding firmly' and commended for. (11:2) Attitudes notwithstanding, they had kept the baptism and the Lord's Table. In the absence of a mandated head covering law, it can only be concluded that it was artificial.

SUMMARY

Nothing in the OT supports the notion that God was offended by outward appearance. Apparently, the Corinthians had, without warrant, invented a head covering standard for corporate worship. They judged and shamed others according to their own opinions about worship. If, indeed a commanded tradition had been violated, then an offense occurred. But without a record of a commanded head covering tradition, no offense was committed.

Anyone not conforming to the expected custom had not been dishonoring those who did. Since 'dishonor' is in the third person, and not in the middle voice, the non-compliant only subjected themselves to the scorn of the compliant legalists. Therefore, non-compliance was not an action of spite or disrespect.

And, most importantly, to this point, Paul has not censured the non-compliant.

---

[73] *Heinrich Meyer's Critical and Exegetical Commentary on the New Testament*, 1 Cor.11:5

11 The Infraction and The Offense

It is obvious that an infraction had occurred in the assembly based on expected traditions. However, to this point, Paul had not censured anyone for a contrary head covering custom. Perceived infractions were entirely based on personal judgments of another's custom. A violation had occurred.

There are basically three views regarding the focus of the head covering violation. Most hold that the physical head is dishonored and others believe that the administrative head is dishonored and still others argue that both are intended.

THE ACTUAL INFRACTION

Because the meaning of the word 'head' can be physical or metaphorical, it is a challenge to stay on the exegetical track. Is Paul referring to the precept of headship just mentioned or is he referring to the physical head?

DISHONORING ONE'S PHYSICAL HEAD

Since the nearest antecedent of the dishonored 'head' is the covered or uncovered 'head', many think that Paul refers to the physical head. Man and woman dishonor their physical head when they did not comply with a widely accepted custom or regulation for worship headwear.

One commentator holding to the view that 'head' in verses 4 and 5 cannot be a reference to administrative headship in verse 3, provides the following illustration,

> "It is more obviously true that a man who acts inconsistently with his station disgraces himself, than that he disgraces him who placed him in that station. A commanding military officer, who appears at the head of his troops in the dress of a common soldier, instead of his official dress, might more properly be said to dishonor himself than his sovereign." [74]

---

[74] Charles Hodge, *Hodge's Commentary on Romans, Ephesians and Colossians*, Please see commentary on 1 Cor. 11:4.

According to Hodge, the man who does not comply with appropriate dress code, does not insult his superior or head; he insults himself only. While this illustrates personal shame, it can hardly be said that his superiors, who trained him, would not be implicated. If a child has bad manners, we naturally wonder if the child is receiving proper guidance from his parents. Secondly, Hodge illustrates the shame caused by the glaring eyes of those who dressed 'properly', including the commanding officer. And, thirdly, soldiers have a dress code; worshippers do not.

A woman in prayer and prophesying without a head covering was equivalent to being shorn and thus she dishonored her physical head. Dishonoring of the 'head' was only possible when a head covering custom was not acceptable. The context indicates that only the non-compliant were dishonored. And, the non-compliant dishonored their own head, not anyone else's.

DISHONORS ADMINISTRATIVE HEAD

Another view teaches that when man covers his head and woman does not, they disgrace their administrative head, that is, man disgraces Christ and woman disgraces man. This assumes that known regulation for worship had been ignored. (11:3) It is believed that 'head' refers to Christ or the husband. (Albert Barnes, Henry Alford) Without an explanation, this is viewed as a temporary imperative linked to the honored custom of that day. (Dr. Thomas Constable) [75]

But without evidence for a previously commanded etiquette for head covering in public worship, diverse customs could not possibly have offended Christ or man by outward appearance even in Christ's day.

'DISHONORS' BOTH PHYSICAL AND ADMINISTRATIVE HEAD

This view holds that both opinions just mentioned are relevant. It is believed by some that man and woman not only dishonor their own physical head, but also their respective administrative head.

SUMMARY

However, since 'dishonors' in verses 3 and 4 are indicative, the view that the worshipper offends the physical head or administrative head by what is worn or not worn on the head is problematic. Without a mandate

---

[75] Some scholars interpret 'head' as the source of embarrassment (physical) while others favor interpreting it as the authority. Constable thinks both are valid. Ellicott taught that Paul was not addressing an actual situation in the church so was merely being proactive. (Ellicott)

for head covering, the violation rests entirely on personal opinion. Indeed, the non-compliant had committed an infraction as far as public opinion was concerned, but had they committed an offense? Who really was responsible for this fellowship fissure? The only remaining group who might be guilty of divisive dishonoring, were among those who complied with the custom.

THE ACTUAL OFFENSE

Whether the non-compliant dishonored their physical head or their administrative head or both, commentators infer that the man who covers and woman who doesn't, had committed an offense. From the context and grammar, however, it becomes apparent that the common notion that the non-compliant caused a division during their worship time must be challenged. (11:3-5) Since no context even hints that a scriptural or apostolic directive existed for worship head wear, the non-compliant should not bear any blame for the shame they experienced.

Who then were the real offenders?

THEIR OWN PHYSICAL HEAD WAS DISHONORED

Indeed, the physical head was the site of the violation. To know the guilty party, the cause of the violation must be known. In this case, some who complied with the custom elevated themselves as judges of inappropriate head wear. Though the man who covered did not comply with expected customs, he did not dishonor others. By covering his head, the man became conspicuous during the service and as such made himself vulnerable to the negative opinions of the compliant. Through no fault of his own the man who covered dishonors his physical head in the presence of others. Those who insisted that everyone comply with the 'required' custom, were responsible for his negative treatment.

These same principles also apply to the woman who didn't cover. It is important to highlight the fact that the non-compliant did not dishonor those who observed the common etiquette for head covering. As regards to their physical head, they did no 'wrong' to anyone else but themselves. They only dishonored their own head, not others.

MAN DISHONORS HIS ADMINISTRATIVE HEAD

But could Paul mean that they were dishonoring their administrative head? Since no biblical warrant specified head wear for prayer and prophesying, the non-compliant man himself could not have sinned against Christ, his administrative Head. If, however, 'head' is indeed a reference to headship, then somehow man praying with his head covered in public was an offense to Christ, his Head. (11:4) But, because he had not broken any commandment, the offender must be someone else. The only other candidate for an offense, then, must be someone who complied with custom as a religious regulation.

Note the following example.

Jesus' Disciples 'Dishonor' Their Head

Contrary to the religious rules of their day the disciples picked some grain on the Sabbath. The Pharisees complained to Jesus, 'Your disciples are doing what is not lawful to do on the Sabbath.' Under the self-righteous glare of the Pharisees, the non-compliant disciples experienced first-hand what it meant to dishonor themselves by failing to abide by Jewish tradition. Apparently, likeminded on Sabbath customs, the disciples had not shamed one another. Similarly, in Corinth those who did not observe the required head covering tradition did not dishonor their 'head' amongst themselves but had personally incurred dishonor from those who <u>differed</u> with them.

Not only had the disciples dishonored themselves, they had also dishonored their teacher as per the Pharisees. (Matt. 12:8) It is noteworthy that the Pharisees' question to Jesus implied that He had failed to teach the 'law' to His disciples. Thus, the disciples' failure to observe the Sabbath rules also dishonored their Rabbi to the Pharisees. By their own action, yet through no fault of their own, the disciples had also 'dishonored' Christ, their Head.

Were the Pharisees justified to incriminate Christ? Jesus provides the answer. Rather than rebuke the disciples, He conferred the blame upon the compliant Pharisees for dishonoring the headship of Christ, declaring that He is the Lord of the Sabbath Day, not them. (Matt. 12:8) Though the disciples disobeyed Sabbath traditions, they were not culpable for how their action had 'dishonored' Christ. The compliant Pharisees 'dishonored' themselves and Christ, by attempting to impose fabricated religious laws. Therefore, the disciples could not be guilty of an offense.

Like the disciples, men in Corinth 'dishonored' themselves and Christ, by not conforming to fabricated religious head covering customs, yet, were not guilty of an offense. Different head covering customs did not offend Christ, but it offended the spiritual elites who unjustly shamed the non-

The Infraction and The Offense

compliant and likewise intercepted the headship of Christ with contrived head covering laws. Jesus was/is **also** Lord of head covering.

The Real Head Covering Offense

The real head covering offense occurred when some in the congregation responded negatively to those who dishonored themselves and Christ by not conforming to the expected contrived tradition for praying and prophesying. Again, there is no evidence or hint that the non-compliant had sinned.

WOMAN DISHONORS ADMINISTRATIVE HEAD

Similarly, every woman who does not conform to the traditional religious head covering custom, dishonors her administrative head, as if she was shaved.

As the Creator of both man and woman, God has set the standard that measures how their respective administrative heads were dishonored. God had created woman to be a suitable helper, not to be a slave or an employee. 'To be' implies that she would know instinctively how to fulfill her role. She wouldn't have to ask Adam, 'what do I do next?' There is no need for man to determine what the woman must do to 'honor' him. Therefore, the view that woman dishonors man as her head, is valid only if she is prevented from being autonomous in her role. Woman becomes an offense to man as her head when man reduces her to function like an automaton, inhibited or even prevented from coming to her own personal conclusions about her work.

The woman with uncovered head had dishonored man even as she functioned in her role, not because she had done anything wrong, but because she had not complied with an imposed behavior. The woman cannot possibly honor the created status of man's headship if he subjugates her to conform to customs with which she feels uncomfortable or disagrees with. Since the woman is autonomous, any dishonor man feels on matters such as head covering, are unjustified. Religious or not, the shame that the woman incurred for not conforming to a contrived custom, occurred because she was judged by others to be inappropriate. Any offense felt by her administrative head was baseless, because the custom regulation had no divine sanction.

Man is honored, as the woman's administrative head, when she freely accepts or rejects customs pertaining to her appearance according to her God-given role in the Scriptures. Woman is autonomous, therefore man's only option is to lead. That's headship! And, as will be dealt with in more detail later, woman also has the right to judge in herself. (11:13)

The following example demonstrate the woman's liberty despite the dishonor she incurred from men.

Is Woman Autonomous?

On one occasion a woman came to Jesus while He was in Bethany to anoint Him with an expensive alabaster flask of oil. Notably, she did this in the presence of men, Jesus' own chosen disciples! (Mat.26:6-13) The disciples in this instance, representative of the woman's head, would have advised otherwise. They excoriated the woman for wasting this precious ointment by pouring it on Jesus' head. Now, who was right? Should the woman have asked 'man', 'Oh please, please, oh may I please anoint Jesus with this oil, please?' It should be apparent that in matters of worship especially, her role is autonomous.

Even if Paul meant that woman's uncovered head 'dishonored' man as her administrative head, she had not sinned. Man was entirely to blame for the shame he had caused the woman.

PHYSICAL HEAD AND/OR ADMINISTRATIVE HEAD

Could Paul have meant that both the physical 'head' and administrative 'head' were dishonored?

Whether the physical head, administrative head or both were the objects of the offense, the head covering custom was contrived by man, not God. Like the disciples thrashing grain on the Sabbath, the non-compliant Corinthians dishonored their physical and spiritual Head.

Secondly, to hold that an offense occurred against the physical 'head' and/or the administrative 'head' is tenable only if the compliant were guilty.

Thirdly, an offense occurred against the physical and/or the administrative head, when the non-compliant were dishonored by not observing the expected custom.

Fourthly, an offense occurred against the physical and/or the administrative head when head covering customs for man or woman violate the principles of moderation.

Fifthly, an offense occurred against the physical and/or the administrative head when head covering customs were imposed, without regard for the autonomy of each man and each woman.

The Infraction and The Offense

Sixthly, 'dishonoring the head' is an offense against the physical and/or administrative head when immature people use head covering as a means to make others look 'spiritual' like them. (14:20)

Conclusions

Therefore, this passage states the opposite of what most commentators allege. There was obviously a conflict, but who was really at fault.

The Custom Does Not 'Dishonor' The Head

The presence or lack of head wear was not the issue; the reaction to another custom was. The custom does not dishonor one's own head or the administrative head – people do.

The Non-Compliant Are Not Indicted

As per OT scripture, Paul had not specified any head covering customs for corporate worship. Neither had he indicted the non-compliant for causing strife.

The Compliant Are Indicted

However, the blame for the conflict belongs only to the 'compliant', who tried to impose their worship customs upon others. By judging others based on their own opinions for acceptable customs for worship, they had committed an offense.

When Is The 'Head' Not Dishonored?

Since no biblical evidence supports the notion that Christ had instituted a head-covering ordinance, the man worshiping with head covered had not personally dishonored Christ, his Head, and neither had the woman worshiping with her head uncovered _personally_ dishonored man, her head. Their different traditions had become infractions based on what _others_ thought.

When Is The 'Head' Dishonored?

The 'head' is dishonored when _others_ impose a custom. The non-compliant man or woman dishonored their head, yet had not offended their head. When someone does not comply with the common custom, he disgraces himself, by exposing himself to the negative opinion of others.

Again, those who did not comply with the expected custom committed an religious infraction, but were not guilty of an offense. And, some who complied with the custom, had not committed a head covering infraction, but were guilty of an offense.

12 The Permission Imperative

The indicatives in verses 3, 4 and 5 may indicate a reason or cause for an imperative to follow, but in themselves they are not commands. But in verse 6, Paul introduces his first imperative concerning woman. Further analysis of the grammar, the background, and the context of these verses with the imperative to follow clearly implicate guilt for wrongdoing.

Having posited that the guilty party were those who demanded that man's head be uncovered and woman's head covered during corporate worship, it would be expected that all of Paul's imperatives would reflect that reality. But, what is Paul's first command?

PAUL'S FIRST HEAD COVERING IMPERATIVE

Following is Paul's first imperative on head covering,

> 6) "For if a woman is not covered – then let her be shorn, and if [it is] a shame for the woman to be shorn or shaven – let her be covered." (11: 6; YLT)

Note that verse 6 does not say or imply, 'Shear off her hair' or 'Put the veil on her head'! It says "let", which means permit. In the aorist imperative middle voice, 'let her be shorn' and present imperative middle voice, 'let her be covered', Paul's imperative has an entirely different meaning than inferred by most commentators.

> "This voice means that the SUBJECT **initiates** the action and **participates** in the results of the action. In other words, the subject is both doing and receiving the action. The middle voice indicates the subject performs an action upon himself or herself (reflexive action) or for their own benefit."[76]

Most imperatives are commands and prohibitions, but a small percentage express permission or consent.[77] Boyer categorized the verbs in 1 Cor. 11:6 as "command or permission".[78] He concludes that,

---

[76] Preceptaustin.org *Greek Quick Reference Guide*
[77] James L. Boyer, *A Classification of Imperatives: A Statistical Study*, p. 37 faculty.gordon.edu
[78] Ibid., p. 40

"The exegesis of the imperative mood, like all exegesis, must be usage-oriented. This study has shown that the imperative mood has a wide latitude of possible meanings from which the exegete must choose the one which, in light of the context, the speaker intended."[79]

Bengal says, "the imperative here is that of permission".[80] But most commentaries incorrectly infer that Paul intends women to wear head covering. Hodge changes this into a command to those who were compliant to make the non-compliant conform, "Let her act consistently. If she wishes to be regarded as a reputable woman, let her conform to the established usage."[81] He recognized the third person but unfortunately, changed the meaning of Paul's command.

THE THIRD PERSON SINGULAR

This permission imperative is in the third person. This command is directed to anyone who wants to govern the woman's haircut or head covering. This is a command to those who had been critical of woman's lack of covering in corporate worship. The command is 'permit', allow or let!! (11:6) This command is <u>not</u> directed at the woman who was violating their custom because it's in the third person. The non-compliant woman is not the target of this imperative.

The uncovered woman is **permitted** to initiate and perform a haircut upon her own head and then cover, if she is embarrassed by everyone's unaccepting glares.

PAUL'S GRAPHIC ADVICE

Had there been a legitimate complaint that a woman's lack of head covering was reason to think of her as one whose head was completely shorn, Paul would have said so. Instead, he commands believers to <u>permit</u> a woman whose head is not covered, to also shave her head!!! Knowing how they had been shaming one another in thought and word, Paul tells them to permit her to do what was to them even more abhorrent! Paul's response is to let the woman do exactly as the rest of them were thinking – shave her own head if she wants to! That's a jaw-dropper!

---

[79] Ibid. p. 54

[80] Johann Albrecht Bengal, *Gnomon of the New Testament*

[81] Charles Hodge, *Hodge's Commentary on Ephesians, Romans and 1 Corinthians*, verse 6

The Permission Imperative

- If a woman is not covered, let her also be shorn. That would magnify the shame in your self-righteous eyes.
- If it is shameful to the woman to be shorn, then let her cover. The man does not decide what is shameful, the woman does.
- If it is not shameful to the woman to be shorn, then she can remain uncovered.

Again, the grammar indicates that though the 'shame' had been initiated by the woman, she had not participated in it. In harmony with this reality, Paul issues this permission imperative to the others. Whether others considered the uncovered woman as one whose head was shaved, was irrelevant. If she doesn't cover, let her shave it all off. Simply put, 'leave the woman alone'.

Paul's Graphic Irony

Sometimes, Paul used sarcasm to emphasize his exhortations.

Irony Of Circumcision

Judaizers had troubled believers by teaching the necessity of circumcision. So stressed was Paul with this false teaching, he says that he wishes that they would become eunuchs. (Gal. 5:11,12)

Sarcastic Of Their Wisdom

Not only had this group of believers been judgmental of each other, they were judgmental of Paul. (4:3) His only concern was how the Lord judged him, not the people. In verse 8, he writes,

> "You are already full! You are already rich! You have reigned with kings without us – and indeed I could wish you did reign, that we also might reign with you!" (4:8; NKJV)

Paul experienced hunger, thirst, insufficient clothing, homelessness, persecution, and defamation. Describing himself and Apollos as fools for Christ's sake, he piles on ridicule with, 'you have become wise in Christ'. (4:9-13) He mocks their 'wisdom' of comfort and status.

Another Sharp Disparagement: Head Covering

As he had resorted to a tinge of irony regarding how he had been treated, he does the same with how the ladies had been treated. It is particularly important to gage apparently unusual admonitions, with this in mind. Consider the paraphrase of verses 5 and 6.

'You think ladies with their heads uncovered during worship are like women who have their heads shaved. I say to you that if a woman's head is uncovered, let her also shear her head. On the other hand, if she is embarrassed, not you, if she is embarrassed, let her cover.'

Since the grammar indicates that Paul addressed the woman's head covering issue in the third person singular, he is writing about what others thought of her. Again, he is not instructing the non-compliant woman.

With this graphic parody, Paul implicates a bunch of worship fashion inspectors by telling them to let the woman without a head covering cut off all her hair. Still dripping with satire, he then advises them that if she is embarrassed, 'let her cover' her bald head.

A woman would not shear her hair publicly. And, since when does she need permission to cover, when embarrassed? Rather than humiliating the ladies, he embarrasses the worship fashion experts who diminished these women. Paul implies, 'If you don't like the woman's uncovered head with hair, then let her shave, let her do the very thing you are thinking.' Of course, knowing that a woman has covered her shorn head, would not make her anymore acceptable to these fashion police.

Summary

Paul does not assume that a woman with short hair is an adulteress.[82] Neither is there any implication in the Bible that a woman's uncovered hair was an indication of sexual prowess. In fact, veiling of women was also a ploy for prostitution! (Gen.38:13-15) As discussed previously, a devout Jewish woman might cut her hair as part of a Nazarite vow or because of grief. It is impossible to reconcile the idea that God would require an external worship fashion with the fact that God looks on the heart. Therefore, to declare to the church that an uncovered woman must be permitted to be shorn and if she is embarrassed, then let her cover, is the only reasoned option Paul has. Whether woman is uncovered with long hair, uncovered and shorn, or covered, all are to be graciously received for the sake of the gospel.

---

[82] Scholars think that Greek and Roman prostitutes had their hair very short. (Thomas Constable, vs.5,6)

13 Man's Obligation

Having dealt with the woman's right to wear or not to wear a head covering, he now directs his attention to the man who covered. Arriving at a correct understanding of Scripture is especially difficult, if the translation is problematic. Translations from the Greek for the English 'ought' in verse 7 are misleading, and also inconsistent when compared with other Scripture.

TRANSLATION ISSUES

Translations invariably tell us that 'man ought not to cover his head'. Is the word 'ought' correct? Note how the same Greek word for 'ought' has the same grammar in another comparable text, yet translated differently.

TRANSLATIONS OF 1 COR. 11:7A
NIV: "A man **ought not** to cover his head..."
ESV: "For a man **ought not** to cover his head..."
NAS: "For a man **ought not** to have his head covered..."

Unfortunately, all translations put the 'not' after 'ought' in this passage. But note how 'not' is placed before the same verb in the following passage where the verb tense and mood are identical.

TRANSLATIONS OF 2 COR. 12:14
NIV: "After all, children **should not have** to save up for their parents, but parents for their children."
ESV: "...For children **are not obligated** to save up for their parents, but parents for their children."
NAS: "...for children **are not responsible** to save up for their parents, but parents for their children."
NKJV: "... for children **ought not** to lay up for the parents, but the parents for the children."

Of the four quoted above, only the NKJV still places the adverb 'not' after the verb, while the others place it before the verb, where the Greek has it. Consequently, it leaves the false impression that it is wrong to provide for parents. If it occurs after, there is only one option: not to save.

But with a proper placement of 'not' before 'obligate', it is clear that children have the option to 'save' or not to save according to need.

The verb translated as 'ought' in 1 Cor. 11:7 and 2 Cor. 12:14, are inconsistent. In both cases this verb *opheilei* is present indicative active, third person singular. And in both cases the adverb 'not' occurs before the verb in the Greek. Had 2 Cor. 12:14 been translated as 1 Cor. 11:7, it would read, 'For the children ought not to save up for their parents...' This translation borders on making saving up for parents a sin and conflicts directly then with the Pharisaical hypocrisy of claiming Corban. (Mk. 7:11) It then wrongly associates the word 'not' with the next verb 'save', instead of the immediate verb 'ought' or 'obligate'.

USE OF 'OUGHT'

While the word translated 'ought' denotes obligation or expectation, English grammar does not permit the use of it in this context. The word 'ought' fails to convey the Greek meaning of obligation or expectation when combined with the negative. In English we say, 'he ought not to do that'. We don't say, 'he is not ought to cover his head; we say, 'he is not obliged to cover his head.'

The English translations misplace 'ought', erroneously linking the negative 'not' to the next verb 'cover' when it should stay linked to the verb 'obliged'. The translations quoted above make covering the head the issue when in actual fact, obligation to cover was the issue, which is why it should be translated, 'a man is not obliged to cover his head...' The negative 'not' should appear before the first verb, 'obligated'.

> "This verse is not saying that a man is to never have his head covered, but rather he is not bound to continually or habitually have it covered." [83]

Placing the negative 'not' after the intended verb alters the meaning entirely. Translating according to grammar and 2 Cor. 12:14 yields the following,

> 'For the same reason, man indeed is not indebted to have his head covered, having the image and glory of God, the woman, however, having the glory of man.'

---

[83] Kevin L. Moore, *Critical Analysis of 1 Corinthians 2:11-16*, 1996 P. 59 Scholars understand correctly that 11:7 is not a prohibition of head covering for man.

In Greek, the word 'not' occurs immediately before 'indebted' or 'owe', not the passive verb 'cover'. (11:7) Taking both the present/active verb for 'owe' and the present/passive verb for 'cover' into consideration, it is again apparent that the man who has his head covered, does so not because he is under obligation, but because he has the right to, having been created in the image and glory of God. Writing in the third person, Paul appeals to the men who were not covering their head, informing them that those who covered, had the freedom to do so.

HEAD COVERING WORSHIP PRACTICES

It was noted in chapter 4 that Greeks worshiped their gods with head uncovered and Romans worshiped their gods with head covered. Apparently, Roman men would uncover their heads in the presence of people of higher rank because they did not want to arouse the jealousy of the gods. Converted Roman men who covered their heads in prayer and prophesying would actually be giving a visual demonstration of having transferred their worship to the one true God. His renewed conscience now constrained him to honor Christ and despise the gods with the same religious traditions he had always known.

Converted Jewish priests would also be inclined to cover.

THE PROBLEM

Apparently, Jewish priests and Roman men continued with their custom of covering their head during prayer, despite the disapproval of others, and the compliant insisted that men worship with head uncovered. One group made head covering customs obligatory; the other group did not. The actual problem was not appearance, but obligation.

THE SOLUTION

Having just stated that woman was permitted not to cover, he affirms the commensurate liberty for man. The plain meaning of the passage is that men were not indebted to cover, which is completely different than men were 'obligated not' to cover or 'ought not' to cover.

The men, for the most part, felt obligated to uncover their head during prayer and prophesying. They felt pressure to comply with religious rulings. They uncovered their head out of a sense of obligation to the wishes of others. On the other hand, the man who covered felt no obligation to cover. He covered his head because it was a personal, heartfelt expression of his worship. He covered because he wanted to.

If there had been a biblical commandment for head covering, Paul would have cited it. Rather than censuring a custom, he exhorted believers, that men as well as women, should not feel obligated to practice someone else's custom. Still sinners, believers are inclined to govern in matters that have no bearing on the growth of the believer.

Paul's solution is that both man and woman may cover or not cover according to personal preference.

Informed By Headship

Some had experienced attempted impositions of a head covering custom in Corinth. It becomes increasingly evident how the principles of headship discussed in chapter 5 are related to Paul's exhortation on head coverings. Paul states, "I would have you know," indicating that they needed to be informed. To know the precept of headship would have mitigated, if not eliminated their unscriptural obligations.

Headship Doesn't Subjugate

By imposing a contrived custom, man had assumed authority to dictate behavior that did not belong to him. Paul, therefore, had highlighted the precept of headship, which stands in stark contrast to governance. The precept of headship forms the basis for how the Corinthian church could effectively solve their head-covering dilemma.

Headship Is Autonomous

By interfering with the autonomy of man or woman in matters having nothing to do with the growth of believers, they had demonstrated their ignorance of the precept of headship. Man is not the woman's dictator, nor another man's dictator. On matters such as outward appearance, no man has the authority to obligate another. Every man's head is Christ, not another man and every woman's head is man, as he follows Christ.

Headship Is Mutually Beneficial

Obligation is selfish. There is no heartfelt concern for the violator's relationship to Christ. Has he repented and believed in Christ? There was no evidence among the Corinthians that they were concerned for the spiritual wellbeing of the perceived 'transgressors'. This is not headship.

Headship Is Not Authoritative

Unfortunately, it is inferred from the word 'dishonors' that the non-compliant man and woman had sinned for supposedly disobeying new

Man's Obligation 85

divinely instituted manners for head covering. Obviously, the passage indicates an offense, but without specific imperatives from Scripture for head covering, no sin can be charged to those who did not comply with the majority. Dictatorial demands for men to uncover bore no resemblance to the principles of headship.

HEADSHIP IS NOT COMPETITIVE

They allowed benign customs, of outward appearance during prayer and teaching, become another cause for division. Their Pharisaical contempt contributed nothing to their sanctification. The 'dishonoring' among themselves was evidence of their lack of good fellowship. Headship is complimentary not divisive and competitive.

SUMMARY

Having taught that even the eating of meat that had been offered to idols makes us neither the better nor the worse, how would mandating a headgear custom for prayer and prophesying help these immature believers? (8:8) Such regulation would be just another outlet for a noxious diet of 'holier than thou'. (14:20)

Knowing Christ's example of how He had received the worship of the woman, who actually washed His feet with her hair, would Paul now obligate worshippers to obey a head covering protocol? Sickened with the virus of legalism, the 'children' among them were spreading spite because they did not like what someone was wearing or not wearing on the head during prayer. Again, Paul informed them that the men who covered did so, not because of a sense of corporate obligation, but rather out of sense of personal desire. They were not the legalists.

Obligations Jeopardizes Witness

Paul was concerned when multiple languages were spoken during their assembly that they would observe some decorum for the sake of witness. (14:23) He didn't outlaw the different languages spoken among them. Similarly, had unbelievers come to one of these meetings and observed that the congregation was hostile to the head covering customs of the Romans or the Jews, their witness would have been negatively affected.

Basis for Judgment

Paul's imperative is 'judge in yourselves'. (11:13) He did not command the church to 'judge others'. Personal autonomy rules out obligation on the head covering issue. But before Paul comes to this conclusion, he presents some additional factors that preclude the supposition that men and women must be covered and men uncovered, during worship.

Man is not obliged to cover for he is the glory of God and the woman is the glory of man. Both, having been created according to their own respective 'glory', make each autonomous.

Since man was not created for the woman, but the woman was created for man, she also has head covering liberty. Note, that it does not say that she was created 'under' man.

The grammar, existing customs and the principles of headship preclude that man is obligated to uncover his head during worship.

14 Image and Glory

The Apostle now reasons for man's and woman's autonomy, based on his created status. 'He (man) is the image and glory of God, but the woman is the 'glory of the man.' (11:7b, KJV) Unfortunately, this statement has been misconstrued to mean that man has an elevated status compared to woman. After all, man is the glory of God but woman is *only* the' glory of man'. She must be inferior because he is the image of God and she is not. But what does this passage say?

IMAGE OF GOD

'Image' is used 23 times in the NT. It is translated as 'likeness', 'representation' and mostly as 'image'. One lexicon understands this to be a metonym "applied to man, on account of his power of command."[84] Since man is not obligated to cover, this definition accords with the autonomous status in which he was created. If woman is not created in the image of God, then we could conclude that only man has the 'power of command'. But, is that really so?

BOTH MAN AND WOMAN WERE CREATED IN THE IMAGE OF GOD

Paul had in mind the creation narrative, where it is stated that "God created man in his own image, in the image of God created he him; male and female created he them." (Gen. 1:27) Both male and female were called 'Adam'. He "called their name Adam in the day when they were created." (Gen. 5:2) Taken from the rib of Adam, Eve, having Adam's likeness, must also possess the image of God. If woman had not been created in the image of God, she would not have been able to bear sons who were. (Gen. 5:3) Therefore, Eve also bore the "image of God".

WHY DID PAUL ONLY REFERENCE MAN AS HAVING GOD'S IMAGE?

Paul makes a notable distinction by omitting the word 'image' in regards to woman. Instead of saying that woman is the 'image and glory of man', he only stated that woman is the 'glory man'. He could not say that 'man is the image and glory of God, but woman is the image and glory of man', because <u>both</u> Adam and Eve were created in the image of God.

---

[84] *Thayer's Greek Lexicon*, https://biblehub.com/greek/1504.htm

Therefore, by omitting the word 'image' in his reference to woman, Paul implies that she, like man, is also created in the image of God. However, as will be discussed in the next section, the mutual image of God in which both man and woman were created is depicted by man as the 'glory of God' and by woman as 'the glory of man'. (11:7)

FEATURES OF THE IMAGE OF GOD IN MAN

God created man in the image of God and he retains the image of God, his sin notwithstanding. (Gen. 1:26; 1 Cor. 11:7) Following are pertinent features of the image of God.

The Capacity to Govern Creation

Part of that image is still displayed in his authority and ability to govern or "have dominion" over creation. God had given Adam a job to do commensurate with his image of God and he would share that work with Eve, also having God's image. He had established a co-regency such that both would share dominion over the earth God had created.

The Capacity for Headship

His teaching here runs parallel to the precept of headship where Paul taught that Christ is the Head of man and man the head of woman. The preexistent relation of God being Head of Christ is characterized in His creation of man and woman. As both God and Christ are not the Head, neither are both man and woman the Head.

As pointed out in chapter five, the members of the trinity do not govern one another. Governance by either man or woman over the other is contrary to the image of God. As the members of the trinity are autonomous, so also are man and woman.

The Capacity For Fellowship

God said, 'Let us make man in our image.' (Gen. 1:26) Man was created first. Since it was not good for man to be alone, He created woman. Despite the Fall, man and woman still had the capacity to show the image of God in fellowship with one another.

SUMMARY

The precept of headship is part of the image of God. Both man and woman were made in the image of God. This shared feature precludes dominance. As the Father does not govern the Son, man must not govern woman.

Obligation is the issue, not appearance, which is why Paul states that man is not obligated to cover his head. (11:7) Since clothes contributed nothing to the image of God when Adam and Eve were created, His image is not something to be attained. Having a worship service, where every man's head was uncovered and every woman's head was covered is therefore unrelated to the image of God or the depiction of it. Outward appearance does not depict the image of God.

Instead of accepting one another for fellowship, they were dishonoring one another by imposing personal opinions for worship upon others. Bearing little resemblance to proper conduct for someone created in the image of God, their sanctimonious attempts at worship only fomented more discord in the fellowship. They obscured the image of God.

GLORY

We come to another word used in verse 7 that pertains to both man and woman. The word is 'glory'. But in this case, the Apostle identifies man as the glory of God and woman as the glory of man.

MEANINGS FOR 'GLORY'

Again, as with all words, the meaning and context of 'glory' help us to understand the intended application. Like 'image', when we think of 'glory', we are inclined to think of outward appearance. According to Thayer's lexicon, the meanings for *doxa* are varied. It can be defined as an estimate, an opinion that results in praise, honor and glory. It is defined as magnificence, excellence, preeminence, dignity and grace. In other contexts, it means majesty. And, it is also described as an observable glorious condition or an exalted state as manifested by Christ on the Mount of Transfiguration. (2 Pet. 1:17,18) Vine's summarizes thusly,

> "Glory, (from *dokeo*, to seem), primarily signifies an opinion, estimate, and hence, the honour resulting from a good opinion."[85]

Having been created in the image of God, both man and woman possess their respective 'glory', as does God. Ultimately, man was created to display the glory of God's righteousness and holiness, yet, despite man's fall in Eden, he is still the glory of God, and woman is still the glory of

---

[85] *Vine's Expository Dictionary of New Testament Words*, (see 'glory')

man. (11:7) Appreciating some of the features of this 'glory', helps to clarify further how Paul would finally resolve the head covering conflict.

GLORY IS A STATE OF BEING

Writing in the present tense, Paul indicates that this 'glory' was not contingent upon human ability or righteousness. (11:7) Despite the sin that all mankind would inherit through Adam, both Adam and Eve retained the 'glory' with which they were created. To bear the image of God with the glory that accompanied it, was intrinsic and unearned. As man did not achieve his 'glory' by obedience to God, neither did woman achieve her 'glory' by obedience to man. It was the natural status in which both were created.

GLORY COMPLIMENTS THE IMAGE

Would it have been a glory to man had God built an automaton with a remote control, instead of woman from Adam's rib? 'Push this button for the learning mode; move the joystick left or right to select the task you want done.' 'You can push another button when you want it to talk, push it again, and it will stop.' 'Push the red button when you want it to cry and the green button when you want it to laugh.' And, God said, 'This is the best I could accomplish from your rib!'

Of course, an automaton could never be a compliment or glory of Adam because it could not possibly bear the image of Adam. If woman is truly the glory of man, she must reflect the image in which she was created. Since the robot's 'intelligence' and work is controlled by man, it cannot be the image of man. The woman created from Adam's rib is a compliment to man because she has her own inherent intelligence, purpose and ability, as does man.

GLORY IS UNIQUE

When Christ returns, He will come in the glory of His Father and in His glory. (Matt.16:27; 25:31) Distinguished by their roles, each Person of the Trinity uniquely depicts the glory of God and shares in each other's glory. (Jn.7:18; 8:50)

Similarly, the glory of God that man is, differs from the glory of man that woman is. (11:8,9) The same inherent independent rights given by God to both man and woman, are exercised according to their different gender created role. The created glory that man and woman are to God, and one another, is unique.

'GLORY' IS NOT SPECIAL RECOGNITION

The man's glory and the woman's glory are different. If man is not obligated to cover in the presence of God, then why should woman cover in the presence of man? Christ, as man's Head, is not glorified by outward appearance and man, as woman's head, is not glorified by her outward appearance. But, in worship, man being the 'glory' of God, does not gain special recognition by removing his head covering.

Paul erased **artificial** distinctions among and between men and women for worship by reasoning (*gar*) that he also was not obligated. (11:7) Consistent with the precept of headship, Paul is clear that 'glory', for man or woman, is a function of personal autonomy.

ONE GLORY IS NOT INFERIOR TO ANOTHER

Man as the glory of God and woman as the glory of man indicates the person each directly compliments. But how are we to understand Paul's distinction between the glories of man and woman? The Greek *de* is a weak adversative conjunction often translated 'but' or 'however'. (11:7)

The Glory of God and Man

Since both man and woman were created in the image of God, man's 'glory' of God is not superior to woman's 'glory' of man. Despite their different roles and order of creation, they are of equal value!

> "There is neither Jew nor Greek, there is neither slave nor free; there is neither male nor female; for you are all one in Christ Jesus." (Ga.3:28; NKJV, emphasis added)

Regardless of ethnicity, status or gender, all believers are one in Christ. No man in Christ is superior to another man or woman and no woman in Christ is inferior to another man or woman. If man has greater 'glory' than woman, then we are not one in Christ.

SUMMARY

The 'glory' of humanity is God's equal affirmation of both man's and woman's distinctive autonomous role. Since neither man or woman were obligated to follow a head covering custom, the 'glory' of which Paul speaks, must flow from a freedom of choice. Since the presence or absence of head covering neither added or subtracted from the man's glory of God and the woman's glory of man, compulsory customs were not from God. Man as the glory of God and woman as the glory of man, precludes artificial and legislated obligations, which only serve to obscure the 'glory' with which each was created. Each, with their unique glory, reflect the image of God, to which head covering customs contributed nothing.

Both man and woman have glory. One 'glory' is not above another. Whether man covers or not, he is the glory of God, not because of appearance but because he is autonomous. Similarly, whether woman covers or not, she is the glory of man, not because of appearance, but because she is also autonomous. God's image is depicted by exercising one's inherent, personal, independent authority to cover or not. Thoughtless, coerced compliance to <u>another</u> custom does not portray the image of God in which both man and woman were created. And, neither does it depict the 'glory' of God or man.

The Corinthians had a cosmetic, external view of 'glory'. Later in his lesson, Paul illustrates 'glory' with outward appearance. Instinctively, a woman knows that long hair is a 'glory' to her. (11:15) Things pertaining to custom, and even nature, have to do with the personal 'glory' or a positive opinion of outward appearance. Man does not need to regulate a woman's appearance; she has the ability and right to determine that for herself.

The 'glory' of both man and woman is a status, which was not acquired by works. It is a created status.

IMAGE AND GLORY

Both man and woman share the <u>image</u> of God equally. Both the <u>glory</u> that man is of God and the <u>glory</u> woman is of man, are unique, complimentary and of equal value.

Therefore a woman's lack of a cloth covering cannot tarnish the glory of man and neither can a man's head covering tarnish the glory of God. (11:8)

15 Fabric Or Authority 'Glory'

Based upon Paul's imperatives that permit both man and woman to cover or not to cover their heads in worship, 'glory' cannot be cosmetic. Man, having the glory of God, is not obligated to follow a contrived custom, and woman, likewise, having the glory of man, is not obligated to follow a contrived head covering custom. (11:7) One important non-cosmetic feature of this 'glory' is identified as authority.

A woman's physical 'glory' was and is her hair, especially long hair. (11:15) Still thought to be insufficient for worship, woman was also to wear a fabric on her head. Paul contrasts this 'glory' fabric head covering the Corinthians expected woman to wear with the authority 'glory' God had already given her. (11:10) As a fabric was not required for man's glory, Paul also reasoned that it was not necessary for woman's glory.

TRANSLATION OF VERSE 10

Paul continues to reason for the personal authority of man and woman with specific reference to creation and procreation. (11:8-12) But, first it is helpful to jump ahead to verse 10 briefly, to reveal a translation discrepancy.

Distortions of Translation

Some translators editorialized the scripture by inserting the word 'symbol'. (NKJV, NAS, ESV) Note the following translation,

> "For this reason a woman ought to have *a symbol of* authority on *her* head, because of the angels." (11:10; NKJV)

'Symbol' is not in the original!

A Literal Translation

The following translation is paraphrased from an Interlinear,

> 'For these reasons, she is obliged to possess authority on her head, through the messengers.' (11:10)

The King James has translated it as 'power on her head'. With a literal translation, incorrect inferences can be recognized and discarded.

Erroneous Symbolism

As stated previously, symbolizing headship with a cloth covering for woman alone is self-refuting. If woman allegedly shows submission to man by wearing a head covering, why should not man also wear a head covering to show his submission to Christ?

But there is more. Clearly, religious Corinthians believed that a cloth head covering was a necessary accessory for the woman's glory in corporate worship. In this context, Paul's response is particularly remarkable. I will come back to this later.

DISTINCTIVE 'GLORY' AT CREATION

Having introduced the subject of the glory of Christ that man is, and the glory of man that woman is, with the word "for", Paul signals that reasons for 'glory' are to follow.

> "For a man is not of a woman, but a woman [is] of man, for a man was also not created because of the woman, but a woman because of the man;" (11:8,9; YLT)

At first glance, it appears that Paul is implying that the relation between man and woman is hierarchal. This notion, however, directly contradicts the liberty he had already granted to both man and woman regarding head covering for worship. These verses contain three primary reasons why man is the glory of God and woman the glory of man.

ORDER – MAN WAS CREATED BEFORE WOMAN

Both Adam and Eve were granted dominion over the earth. Territory does not define 'glory'. (Ge. 1:27,28) But man is the 'positive estimation' of God because He uniquely formed him from the dust of the ground and breathed into his nostrils the breath of life. (11:9; Gen.2:7) He was first.

MEANS – BOTH MAN AND WOMAN WERE MADE BY GOD

On the other hand, woman, having been created from Adam's rib is the complimentary appraisal of man. (11:8b; Gen.2:21) God made her to be the glory of man. God is the originator of the glory of both man and woman. (11:8; Ge. 2:23)

PURPOSE – WOMAN WAS MADE FOR MAN

God's reason for creating woman in Genesis 2:18 is probably the most misunderstood citation. The man was not created to be woman's commander-in-chief. She was created as an autonomous assistant. Woman

Fabric or Authority 'Glory'

is the glory of man by her complimentary help and companionship. (11:9; Gen. 2:18)

SUMMARY

Order, means and purpose of the creation of man and woman shows how man is the glory of God and how woman is the glory of man. (11:7) Evidently, the Corinthians deduced that creation order, means and purpose made the glory of man greater than the glory of woman. There is no hint that outward appearance contributed to either the man's or the woman's glory. Neither was man's 'glory' superior to the woman's.

THE WOMAN'S 'GLORY' OF AUTHORITY

Man assumes he has greater 'glory' because he was created first, that he was the source of the woman and that she was created for man. Having stated that she is the glory of man, Paul then contrasts her glory with man's glory in terms of the order, means and purpose of her creation. (11:7-9) Do these differences require she wear a head covering? (11:10)

HER GLORY IS AUTHORITY, NOT FABRIC

Rather than obligating the woman to have a fabric head covering, Paul specifically obligates her to have authority on her head! Authority! Not cloth! Instead of an external, artificial, material symbol of glory, he informs the church that woman needs authority on her head – not cloth.

Example of Woman's Authority

It has been argued variously that in Jesus' day all the women appeared in public with a head covering. Had that been true, it would be expected that Jesus would have reprimanded the woman who washed and anointed His feet. (Matt. 26:13) The disciples did not insult the woman for her lack of covering. (Jn. 12:1-8). This woman was publicly displaying her affection for her Lord by wiping His feet with her hair! She asked no one for permission to remove her head covering, if indeed she had been wearing any, and under her own 'authority' worshiped Him. If Jesus did not censure this woman, why do we?

THE WOMAN IS OWED AUTHORITY

With the word *opheilei*, meaning obligation or indebtedness. Paul implies that something in her possession had been withheld from woman. In this case, she was being denied the right to exercise her own authority, regarding head covering. Paul's recognition of the woman's inherent authority, further explains why he did not add religious rules for head covering. (11:6,7) Believers have no right to dictate customs for either man or woman. In accord with the precept of headship at the beginning of Paul's exhortation, the woman is autonomous. To be the 'glory of man', she must function as her own authority, not as the 'robot of man'.

'Glory' and Obligation Do Not Mix

Obligation is not part of glory. Every man expresses the glory of God by exercising his option to cover or not to cover. Similarly, every woman expresses the glory of man by exercising her option to cover or not to cover. Imposed personal obligations is not a feature of the 'glory' of the man or woman. Woman was not part of Adam's dominion.

Summary

Any woman subjugated to the arbitrary demands of a custom for corporate worship, obscures the image of God and glory of man with which they were both created. She is robbed of her rightful authority.

Mutual 'Glory'

Having assured woman that she was obliged authority 'on her head', Paul returns to the subject of origins. Indeed, man's and woman's created order, means and purpose are different. But, is there a 'glory' that both man and woman share alike? Paul explains,

> "But neither [is] a man apart from a woman, nor a woman apart from a man, in the Lord, for as the woman [is] of the man so also the man [is] through the woman, and all things [are] of God." (1 Cor.11:11,12; YLT)

Man And Woman Are Interdependent

Still, on the subject of personal authority, Paul completes his argument. Indeed, the first man was directly created by God, before woman existed and formed the woman from Adam's rib. (11:8,9) But, lest any man think he has unilateral authority over woman because Adam was created first, he reminds believers that since creation, without each other, man and woman would not exist. Though the first woman came from the first man, every man since, came from a woman. (11:11)

Whether by creation or procreation, the 'glory' of the existence of man and woman is the same. Therefore, man cannot claim power or authority <u>over</u> woman.

Man And Woman Have God As Their Authority

Another 'glory' shared by man and woman is their common creator. Whether from the dust of the ground or the rib of man, God made them both at creation. Despite the fact, that man was created first, neither could he exist apart from God.

'In The Lord'

As God had planned that woman would be taken from the man in creation, so He had also planned that every man since then, would come from the woman. It was just as much 'in the Lord' that every man after Adam would come from woman, as it was 'in the Lord' for the first woman to come from man. (Ge. 1:28)

'All Things Are From God'

The Corinthians had been directing the affairs of corporate worship as if they could speak authoritatively for God. Having dismissed their quest for authority based on man's supposed ascendancy, Paul points to the only One who is ascendant. All things belong to God. (11:12) Or, literally, 'All matters of God'. All things belong to God.

Since 'all things are from God', He is also the personal and final authority of woman, as He is of man. (11:11,12) Man is not a substitute for God's authority.

Personal Authority

From eternity past, God precedes everything and for that reason has unilateral authority. But, since Adam, every man was preceded by woman, his mother. Thus, he demolishes the presumption that because man was created first, he has an inherent governing authority over woman. Neither man or woman can claim ascendant authority based on who came first. Having made them both in His image, they share dominion over creation as co-regents. Both, having God as their authority, are able to exercise personal authority harmoniously.

Therefore, Paul could say, 'Judge in you yourselves.' (11:13)

One Essential Worship Covering

After Adam and Eve ate from the forbidden tree, their eyes were opened to their nakedness. Ashamed, they resorted to their own ability to remedy the problem. Unable to trust the efficacy of their own hand made fig leaf garments, they still hid from God. Despite their work to make themselves acceptable in the sight of their righteous and holy Creator, their sin was still as exposed as it was before. So, God made garments out of skin for man and woman to portend that a life had to be taken, blood had to be shed, to provide them with the remedy for lost fellowship with God. As sinners, the material of this garment must be the same for man as it was for woman. The same price was paid for man, as was for woman. In acceptable worship, both man and woman must wear the same garment of righteousness provided by Christ through His shed blood. Indeed, both man and woman needed a covering – the same covering.

To suppose, therefore, that the genders must somehow be distinguished by a particular custom in worship, obscures the very essence of how sinners are permitted to enter the presence of God. Both man and woman must be dressed in His righteousness for acceptable worship. It is the same garment for both man and woman. Therefore, man's status as the glory of God and woman's status as the glory of man are not compromised by the presence or absence of fabric head covering.

God's worship covering for man and woman was exactly the same!!

Conclusions

Paul's reference to the creation narrative is not incidental. The 'glory' of man and woman have differences and similarities. Both man and woman have 'glory' as an inherent attribute. Since neither is obligated to submit to head covering protocol, each having their own 'glory', implies that both are autonomous under God's final authority. The woman is obliged to have authority-'glory', instead of a fabric. It is an essential compliment for her spiritual head covering.

Having established that the woman must have "authority" on her head, she must also know how her authority is informed. By what means can she know that she is exercising her authority correctly?

16 The Messengers

Perhaps some of the strangest commentary on this passage pertains to the identity of 'angels'. Most, believing that this is a reference to heavenly beings, teach that Christian men and women need to carefully observe protocol for the sake of these heavenly beings who are present with us during our worship services. Head coverings are alleged to help heavenly beings identify male and female worshipers. Since there is no indication in Scripture that man and woman are to oblige 'angels' by what is worn during worship, how are we to understand this reference to 'angels'?

Again, we encounter a translation issue.

ERRONEOUS TRANSLITERATION

This time instead of adding a word such as 'symbol', translators have transliterated the Greek *aggelos* with the word 'angels'. In today's vernacular, the first meaning that comes to mind when reading 'angel' is heavenly being. But that is not the essential meaning of the Greek.

WHAT DOES 'ANGEL' MEAN?

The Greek word *aggelos* means 'messenger' – always.[86] Similarly, the Hebrew *malak* always means 'messenger' or 'ambassador' – always, not 'angels', as it is usually editorialized. The name for the Prophet, Malachi, means 'messenger of the Lord'. The identity of the messenger(s) must be determined from the context.

WHO ARE THE MESSENGERS OF THE BIBLE?

A review of some NT references to *aggelos* is necessary for a proper exegesis of Paul's text. The messengers (angels) of the Bible are most often heavenly beings, but sometimes they are human beings or impersonal agents.[87]

---

[86] When Paul states that even if he was able to speak in the languages of 'men and of messengers', it does not necessarily mean heavenly beings. Every time heavenly beings spoke, it was in the language the Jews actually knew. He may have meant ambassadors who were able to convey messages from one government to another in the language of that country. (13:1) Ambassadors would need to speak multiple languages.

[87] Merrill F. Unger, *Unger's Bible Dictionary*, Moody Press, 1976, p. 52

'ANGELS' REFERENCED IN THE NT

Following are instances of messengers in the NT.

- Rahab received 'angel' messengers from Joshua. (Jas.2:25)
- Each of the churches in Revelation 2 and 3 had an 'angel'. Clearly the context indicates that these were not heavenly beings.
- John the Baptist is Christ's messenger 'angel'. Quoting from the OT, Jesus stated that God would be sending His messenger 'angel' ahead of Him (Mal. 3:1; Matt. 10:11). It is clear that John the Baptist was a messenger- prophet. (Lk.7:27,28)
- John the Baptist had sent messengers (angels) to Jesus for some clarification on His identity. (Lk.7:22-24) Jesus had told John's messenger (angels) to return to John and inform him about the miracles that Jesus was doing.
- Jesus sent messengers (angels) ahead of Him to Samaria. (Lk.9:52)
- Jesus had sent messengers ahead to Samaria. (Lk.9:51,51)

HEAVENLY BEING 'ANGELS'

It is easily determined that the 'angel of the Lord' that appeared to Joseph in a dream was not a human being. (Matt.1:20,24; 2:19) Gabriel was a heavenly messenger to Mary. (Lk.1:26) At the end of the age, messengers (angels) shall separate the just from the wicked. (Matt. 13:49) And, other 'angel' references clearly indicate non-human participation in the event described. With the phrase 'angels of heaven' it is implied that there are other 'angels' that are not from heaven. (Matt. 24:36)

HUMAN BEING 'ANGELS'

There are two primary human messengers (angels) of note in the OT. They are the priests and the prophets, both known in the Hebrew as *malak*, that is, 'messenger' also translated 'angel' elsewhere.

Priests

In the OT, priests were charged with the responsibility to make known to the people what God had spoken through his Prophets. They are called 'messengers' (angels).

> "For the lips of a priest should keep knowledge, and people should seek the law from his mouth; for he is the messenger (angel) of the Lord of hosts. (Mal. 2:7, NKJV, brkts. added)

By means of the 'budding rod', descendants of the sons of Aaron were designated to be the priest-teachers of the land. They would perform the temple offerings and teach Israel. (Num. 17; De. 33:10; Hos.4:6; Ezra 7:10) The priests were to teach the Law that God had given the people through the Prophets.

Prophets

Again, as indicated above, the name 'Malachi' means 'messenger of the Lord'. It must be emphasized that Prophets were also known as 'messengers.' The same Hebrew word *malak*, translated as 'messenger' or 'ambassador' in a few places, is mainly, erroneously translated as 'angel'. A prophet is one who delivers a message, hence, according to the Bible, a messenger. Prophets are messengers. (2 Chron.36:14-16)

WHO ARE THE MESSENGERS OF AUTHORITY?

The Apostle Paul did not command the woman to wear a 'symbol', but rather to be in possession of real authority. The source of this special authority is delivered through 'messengers'. But, which messengers?

The message of the priests was subject to the message of the Prophet-messengers. (2 Chron.36:14-16) The priests had sinned by superseding the authority of the prophet-messengers God had sent to Israel. So, who are these messengers in Corinth?

THE MESSENGERS SPOKE WITH AUTHORITY

By God's own authority, He had also delegated the means by which His truth could be known. It was conferred through the messengers. Peter writes that holy men of God spoke **not** by their own will, but as they were moved by the Holy Spirit. (2 Pe.1:20,21)

THE MESSENGERS COMMUNICATED TO MAN AND WOMAN

Messages were always equally understandable by both man and woman. She has the right to appeal directly to the words of authoritative messengers.

THE MESSENGERS WERE PROPHETS

"The messengers" of the Lord were Prophets. (Heb. 1:1) They delivered the truth from God about sin, punishment, redemption, repentance, faith, and salvation to Israel. These prophets had authority by the word of the Lord. But the Prophets died, then what?

The prophets had scribes to write down their prophecies, and so provide multiple copies for distribution to the people. At the first oral, the word of the Lord was also recorded.

When the Bereans checked the Scriptures to confirm Paul's message, they consulted the Scriptures, which were written by the Prophet-messengers. Rather than checking the Scriptures as the Bereans had, the Corinthians attempted to create their own sense of worship, without the authority of the 'messengers'.

An example of the linkage between authority and messenger is Aquila and Prisca, who together informed Apollos how to teach the Word more accurately. (Ac.18:26-28) Paul alluded to the message of the Prophet messengers when he exhorted the Corinthians not to exceed what is written. (1 Cor. 4:6) Every woman's authority to refuse religious regulation and false doctrine always was the Scriptures, written by God's Prophet-messengers.

Summary

God had created woman to be a suitable helper for man, yet, neither man or woman have unilateral authority over the other. The woman's supportive role does not preclude her autonomy. Her authority entitles her to resist any suggested or mandated practice forced upon her by appealing to the messengers, the written word of God. She also has authority to verify the teachings about faith and practice – through the messengers, the inspired writers of the word of God. This is her ultimate authority, the same as it is for man.

The woman is not mandated anywhere in Scripture to signal her 'subservient' role to man with head covering, for the sake of heavenly beings.

17 Judge Your Own Customs

Having shown by reason of creation and procreation, that neither man or woman exist by their own authority, he resolves the head covering conflict with an imperative that applies to both. Consistent with the principle of autonomy, for both man and woman, Paul now exhorts believers to judge for themselves.

'In You Yourselves Judge'

Paul's imperative is literally, "in your own selves judge ye". (11:13a; YLT) As discussed previously, in the absence of the middle voice for the verb 'dishonors', it is implied that others participated in disgracing those deemed inappropriate. (11:4,5) He does not say, 'among yourselves judge others', which is what they had been doing.

How Are We To Judge?

Each person, having their own authority, is free to judge in himself or herself what their head covering practice should be. Paul calls for a remedy for their conflict with a couple rhetorical questions.

The First Rhetorical Question

Paul engages believers with a question he expects each to answer for themselves. Specific to the woman's worship custom, he asked,

'is it proper for woman to pray to God uncovered?' (11:13b)

One group would answer, 'no', the other, 'yes'.

The 'No' Response

From his review of Corinthian behavior, we know that the problem was caused by those who answered, 'no, it's not proper. . .'. Doubtless, Paul framed the question to highlight the 'custom', which was the primary cause of division among them. Those who answered 'no', believed that it was not proper for woman to pray uncovered.

The 'Yes' Response

The Corinthians who had been subjected to dishonor would have answered 'yes'. It was okay for woman to pray uncovered.

Paul's Implied 'Answer'

What was Paul's answer? It should be noted that Paul did not say whether the answer should be 'no' or 'yes', however, we now know from the context of the entire passage, what his answer would be. With the imperative to 'judge in yourselves', he affirms the personal right of the woman to choose her own custom. In order to 'judge in yourselves', the answer to this question can be 'no' or 'yes', depending on one's own opinion. She is free to ignore the judgment of others.

It is important to note that the word 'proper' does not imply that the woman sins, if she is not wearing a head covering. (11:13b) 'Proper' must be understood in the context of the 'dishonor' some conferred on women, who were uncovered during prayer and prophesying. As far as God is concerned, they had not been 'improper'.

THE SECOND RHETORICAL QUESTION

With a second question, Paul shows how nature has a bearing on custom differences between man and woman,

> 'Does not even nature itself teach you that if a man indeed has long hair, it is a dishonor to him, however, a woman, if she has long hair a glory it is to her?' (11:14,15a; Biblehub.com, interlinear NT)

Paul appeals to common knowledge. Everyone knows that nature teaches woman's hair length. Everyone also knows that nature teaches woman that long hair compliments her beauty. Everyone knows that nature teaches that long hair does not compliment man's appearance. Therefore, it is nature that determines differences, not custom.

Since nature teaches woman whether she has sufficient hair, she will also know if she needs a fabric covering for worship. If woman's head is uncovered during prayer, nature has confirmed that her covering is sufficient. When woman is wearing a head covering during worship, by nature she feels that her hair or lack of hair is insufficient.

WHAT IS MEANT BY NATURE?

Paul noted that differences in hair length is taught by nature. (1 Cor. 1:14,15) In his letter to the Romans, he articulated how man descends into abject immorality by ignoring nature.

Despite the Fall, 'that which may be known of God is manifest in them.' (Rom. 1:19-20) It is natural to deduce that the creation of the world could not possibly have been made by images of corruptible man and animals. Yet, contrary to nature, man defaults to vain imaginations and worships the created instead of the Creator. (Rom. 1:21-23) Then God gives them over to the vile passions of their heart, whereby they 'change the natural use into that which is against nature.' (Rom. 1:26, 27) Homosexuality is not natural. Until God "gives them over", everyone has an inherent sense of what is right. In this context, human nature harmonizes with biblical morality.

Prior to their conversion, Paul tells Ephesian believers that they were dead in their trespasses and sins. (Eph. 2:1) Then, he reminds them that 'they were by nature the children of wrath.' (Eph. 2:3) In this context, man's 'nature' is an offense to God.

One nature is a good teacher; the other nature is the reason for God's wrath. Man has a human nature and a spiritual nature. Despite the Fall, man still possesses the moral evidence of the Law in his human nature. However, since the Fall, man has acquired an evil spiritual nature over which human nature has no power. Human nature cannot decide to get man out of this spiritual dilemma; it can only inform.

As per the head covering conflict, Paul is speaking about human nature, not spiritual nature.

GUIDANCE BY HUMAN NATURE

Head covering customs emerged from human nature, apart from any biblical mandate. Unlike the 'traditions' of Baptism and the Lord's Table, <u>head covering</u> was not a '<u>delivered</u>' custom. Head covering, as with hair length, is a <u>natural</u> impulse of human nature; baptism and the Lord's Table are not.

NATURE IS UNIQUE TO GENDER

As with head covering, God had not legislated hair length, yet man and woman respectively, instinctively conform to an unwritten code taught to them through human nature, not Scripture. The presence or absence of head covering is natural, therefore, not the issue. However, wearing head covering contrary to one's gender, would have been an issue.

Informed by nature, man and woman know what their hair length ought to be. Society, then and now, does not consider long hair for man a cosmetic improvement. Long hair is not personal 'glory' to man, as it is for woman. Paul teaches that a woman knows by nature that hair is her 'glory'. Women abhor being bald. This is taught by nature, not custom.

NATURE IS SUBJECTIVE

Though men mostly have their hair shorter and women have their hair longer, each man and woman still have their own opinion of what short hair is, and what long hair is. Even when hair lengths and head coverings change, nature is still the teacher by default, not customs.

SUMMARY

Man makes customs; God created human nature. Normal expression of human nature was interrupted by imposing customs. In the absence of biblical instruction, Paul advised to 'judge in themselves', according to human nature, not customs. Human nature governs human custom. Therefore, to impose unwanted customs upon individuals violates human nature and Scripture.

'HAIR' OR 'COVERING'?

We come now to the last half of verse 15 where Paul gives further reasons for the woman's liberty,

> 'For the long hair instead of a covering is given to her.' (11:15b; from biblehub.com)

COVERING AND COVER

Some rightly hold the woman's right not to wear head covering by arguing that 'covering' is hair, not fabric. But 'covering' (*peribolaiou*) is defined as a mantle, or a cloak: something that is wrapped around; it is not hair. (11:15) The word 'cover' (*katakalyptetai*) used in verse 6, is a verb. By definition and context, the thought expressed by both the Greek verb and the noun implies the donning of a fabric.

'INSTEAD OF A COVERING' OR 'FOR A COVERING'?

Scholars disagree on the translation of *anti*.[88] Some say it should read, '...hair is given to her <u>for</u> a covering.' Others say is should be translated, '...hair is given to her <u>instead</u> of covering.' (11:15b) Elsewhere *anti* is translated 'for' but the meaning is 'opposite', 'instead of', 'in place of'.[89]

---

[88] A Kevin L. Moore, *Critical Analysis of 1 Corinthians 2:11-16*, 1996 P. 79. Also, *Coffman's Commentaries on the Bible*, on verse 5 he argues that there is no 'intrinsic meaning that suggests covering material or object covered.' But the context suggests otherwise.

[89] *Thayers' Lexicon*
https://biblehub.com/greek/473.htm

Some think that the woman's greater hair length is nature's way of showing that a cloth covering is expected. Note Kevin L. Moore's reference to Brown and Bauer,

> In 1 Cor. 11:15 Paul's point is not that a veil is superfluous for a woman since nature has given her hair in place of a covering, but rather, arguing analogically, he infers from the general fact that "hair has been given to serve as a covering"... that the more generous supply of hair that a woman has when compared with a man shows the appropriateness of her being covered... (Brown 3:1179; cf. Bauer 73) [90]

This sounds plausible. But the problem with his interpretation ignores the permission imperatives. Secondly, it really does say 'in place of' or 'instead' of a covering. It does not say, 'as a covering'. When translated correctly, it is easy to see that because the woman regarded her hair as her 'glory', it would be natural for her to regard her hair as an adequate covering. In effect, Paul again affirms her right not to wear an artificial covering. If she is shorn, then it is likely she would want a cloth covering to avoid embarrassment.

HER 'GLORY' PRECLUDES ARTIFICIAL COVERING

At the beginning of his teaching, Paul exhorts the church, <u>not her</u>, to let a woman who is not covered to also be shorn, implying that she had hair. (11:5,6) If her hair is shorn and she feels self-conscious about it, then, let her cover. The choice for a covering was entirely hers. Paul reasons that the woman knows by nature that she needs hair to avoid embarrassment. (11:14) If, in her opinion, she has sufficient hair, nature 'teaches' her that she does not require a fabric covering.

This is about feeling personal embarrassment; it is not about embarrassing anyone else! Nothing in verses 13 to 15 suggest that inappropriate hair length is an embarrassment to God in corporate worship. By nature, she 'judges in herself' whether her hair is a 'glory' for herself. Paul echoes a previous imperative, that women might not feel the necessity to cover their head with a fabric, because, for them, hair serves as sufficient covering. Therefore, if a woman having long hair, is not ashamed, why should she cover up what is a 'glory' to her with a fabric?

---

[90] Kevin L. Moore, *A Critical Analysis of 1 Corinthians 2:11-16*, 1996 P. 79.

Her 'Glory' Is Known By Means Of Her Nature

Knowing by nature that her own hair is already a 'glory' to her, she is at liberty to regard her hair as covering in place of a fabric. This is about her 'glory', not about what someone else thinks her 'glory' ought to be. Having been taught by means of her nature, that hair is her 'glory', she has no need to add 'glory' with more head covering.

Hair Length Is Governed By Nature

Styles notwithstanding, every woman has her own sense of what the appropriate length of her hair ought to be. Likewise, man's hair length is guided by his own sense of propriety. Each one is to judge in himself or in herself the head covering according to one's own natural personal preference, not someone else's.

If a woman has had a longstanding tradition of covering for public worship, she will likely be uncomfortable without a head covering. But whatever her custom, she is to be left to her own discretion. Since God does not stipulate the presence or absence of head covering as a ticket to worship, everyone is free to practice their preference. Natural sensibilities will govern what is appropriate for each. If nature can teach a woman what her hair length ought to be, then she will certainly know if her head covering compromises her 'glory'. So, Paul affirms physical nature as the guide for woman regarding head covering, not religious regulations.

How Are We To Judge?

Paul provides believers an understanding of how believers can judge what is appropriate for themselves.

Judge According To Your Own Preference

Again, Paul uses the Greek word *doxa* glory to refer to long hair as the glory of the woman. This is not to be confused with the 'glory of God' or the 'glory of man'. (11:7) Paul specifically states that for a woman to have long hair it is a glory <u>to her</u>, not to man. She has long hair because it compliments her appearance. (11:14,15) Someone else's opinion about what her 'glory' ought to be, is irrelevant.

Outward appearance has no cosmetic connections to either the glory of man or the glory of God. Long hair on a man is not relevant to anyone's honor but his own. Similarly, head covering is solely a matter of one's personal sense for complimentary attire in any public venue, corporate worship notwithstanding.

Judge Your Own Customs

JUDGE IN YOURSELVES ACCORDING TO NATURE

To suggest, as commentators do, that head covering was a moral issue is preposterous. Paul knew the Scriptures cited earlier about the requirements for masculine and feminine clothing and would have referenced them had that been the issue. For a woman to have uncovered hair, whether in the church or in the public square, was not an act of seduction.

Should we wear uniforms to church? Custom control endeavors to make people wear or do the same thing. Nature allows for individual expression.

JUDGE IN YOURSELVES ACCORDING TO PERSONAL PRACTICE

A Roman or a former Jewish priest would not have the same natural inclinations for head wear as would the Greek. Some in the church had acquired a personal sense of propriety from ethnic and religious background. To violate one's longstanding practice is like doing what is contrary to nature.

What would these Corinthians say to the woman who publicly worshiped Jesus by washing His feet with her hair? This was a public act and it was worship!! Were the supposed 'angels' able to tell the difference between her, Jesus, the disciples and the Pharisees?

As each man and especially woman is self-conscious about hair length, so also let it be with the observance of a custom such as head covering. If a woman is present who has shaved her head for any reason, let her be! (11:6) Be concerned for the salvation of her soul first! After that, God by His Holy Spirit and the Word will adjust her customs as He deems necessary. She has the right to judge in herself.

SUMMARY

Paul wants them to be careful not to be governed by religious imposition of artificial customs. If nature can teach men and women simple habits like hair length, it can also serve as your teacher on personal matters such as head coverings. The common custom for man to have short hair and woman to have longer hair was not prescribed in a book somewhere, certainly not the Scriptures. Paul did not want them to be held in bondage to man-made religious customs for head covering. They were to be informed by their own natural inclinations, not made-up regulations. (Col.2:20-22) To judge in oneself, precluded the judgments of others. Both man and woman were free to practice their own custom.

As part of her innate sense of feminine propriety, woman is inclined to enhance her appearance with long hair, not head covering. Some in the Corinthian church were trying to impose a custom upon her that she might not consider a 'glory' to her. Why cover what God created to be a normal, moderate and natural expression of her womanhood? (11:15) 'In yourselves judge', does not mean that others can decide for the woman whether to cover her head or not!! It means exactly what it says, 'in yourselves'. This is not subject to a majority vote, or a church board of directors!

Instead of a Head Covering

Now, if 'even' nature teaches what the length of hair should be to avoid the dishonor of others, then it follows that nature also teaches woman that her hair has been given instead of a covering. The same principle applies to a fabric covering. If, in her opinion, she thinks that her hair might detract from her 'glory', then, naturally she will find it necessary to don a fabric.

At the outset of Paul's lesson, he alluded to the possibility of a woman who might be present with very short hair and in the presence of others who had long hair and might feel embarrassed. In that case, she had the option to cover if she so desired.

Head covering itself was not a moral issue, however, the act of judging others on this issue was. Paul left it up to each person to 'judge in themselves', according to nature. (11:13-15)

JUDGE YOURSELF, NOT OTHERS

Paul does not legislate appropriate hair length or head coverings. Each have the right to judge their own hair dilemma, not others. Since God Himself had instituted the Nazarite vow, judging others for 'improper' hair length is actually improper. (Jud.13:5,14) Both Paul and Samson violated 'nature' by growing long hair, yet had not sinned. Paul had given specific reason for judging the immorality of others. (1 Cor. 5) But, the absence or presence of head covering had nothing to do with sin!

18 'No Such Practice'

By way of a brief review, the grammar pertaining to those who dishonored their head is not in the middle voice, indicating that they only initiated the action but did not participate in the result of their action. Secondly, the third person indicates that Paul was speaking about these head covering 'violators', not to them. And, thirdly, whether disgracing their physical or administrative head, the non-compliant violators had not been commanded to stop!

Having shown that man-made worship customs do not supersede nature, Paul now concludes the matter with one short statement,

> "But if any man seem to be contentious,[91] we have no such custom, neither the churches of God." (11:16; KJV)

'Seems' can also be translated as 'appears'. Both the ESV and the NAS translate *dokei* as 'inclined'. The word 'custom' can also be translated as 'practice' or 'tradition'.

INTERPRETIVE CHALLENGE

Commentators are not united on the identity of 'custom'. Some commentators hold that 'no such custom' pertains to a practice of contentiousness. But, the majority hold that 'no such custom' is the practice of a woman praying uncovered, based on an assumed negative answer to the rhetorical question, 'Is it appropriate for a woman to pray uncovered?' (11:13) Does 'no such practice' pertain to the practice of contention or to a practice of contentious head covering?

MEANING OF PRACTICE?

The Greek word for 'practice' is used only three times in the NT. Vine's understands this noun to mean "force of habit". The Greek for 'practice' indicates that this was not just a casual occurrence.[92]

---

[91] This is an ellipsis where the noun is not provided. 'Contentious' is an adjective used as a noun. For example, in, 'A parking spot is reserved for the disabled,' the noun for the adjective 'disabled' is not provided but is understood to be a person.

[92] The Jews had a 'practice' that a criminal be released at the Passover. (Jn. 18:39) Idolatry is a 'practice'. (1Cor.8:7)

"To which "custom" does Paul refer? The word he uses is sunetheia, meaning "custom, habit, usage" (Bauer 821). This involves more than a mere "practice" (prasso). It is a customary or habitual practice; an established custom (cf. H. Moulton 389).[93]

Custom is a repeated pattern of behavior. What was it?

THE TWO 'PRACTICES'

Was Paul addressing the 'practice' of judging one another for not complying with an accepted custom?

Or, was Paul addressing the 'practice' of men who were covering their head, or women, who weren't?

HOW MANY CUSTOMS ARE THERE?

The two prevailing customs in the Corinthian church were that man's head was to be uncovered and woman's covered during worship. (11:4-7) Two competing customs were the opposite: men covered, women uncovered. There were four customs.

At the end of Paul's teaching on head coverings, he declares that 'we have no such practice'. Since *synetheian* is singular, he could only be referring to one custom, or one 'such custom'.

CONTENTION OR COVERING?

What then is the referent of 'no such custom'. Does 'custom' refer to habitual contentiousness or does it refer to an actual head covering practice? The following explains these two views,

> "Calvin, and many of the best modern commentators, give a different view of this passage. They understand the apostle to say, that if any one seems to be disputatious, neither we nor the churches are accustomed to dispute. It is not our wont to waste words with those who wish merely to make contention. The only reason assigned for this interpretation, is Paul's saying we have no such custom; which they say cannot mean the custom of women going unveiled. But why not? The apostles and the churches constituted a whole neither the one nor the other, neither the churches nor their infallible guides, sanctioned the usage in question. Besides, no other custom is mentioned in the

---

[93] Kevin L. Moore, *A Critical Analysis of 1 Corinthians 2:11-16*, 1996 P.81-82

context than the one which he has been discussing. "If any one appear contentious," is not a custom and suggests nothing to which the words such a custom can naturally refer."[94]

Most commentators hold that 'no such custom' refers to a woman praying with uncovered head[95], that the referent of 'practice' is Paul's question regarding the propriety of woman to pray uncovered. (11:13,16)[96] It is argued that Paul is cutting off all future disputes on the custom of head coverings based on only one acceptable assumed answer to the rhetorical question, 'Is it appropriate for a woman to pray uncovered?' (11:13) Supposing that the answer must be 'no', it is believed that the Apostle's 'no such custom' was the woman praying uncovered. Does 'custom' refer to a supposed accepted protocol for head covering, which was the cause of the contention? A minority hold that the 'custom' referred to, was 'contentiousness'.[97] Does 'no such practice' (custom) refer to the custom of the woman having her head uncovered or does it refer to the custom of being contentious? Or, might there be two ways of understanding this passage?

DOES PAUL MEAN A HEAD COVERING PRACTICE?

It is alleged that 'to be contentious' implicated anyone who would dispute Paul's supposed instruction that woman should cover.[98] This mistaken supposition is based on the notion that Paul had previously 'delivered' a head covering tradition. Given Paul's permission imperative for woman, the declaration that man is not obligated to cover and his imperative to 'judge in yourselves', this view is untenable. From the beginning of this passage, Paul had <u>not</u> indicted the non-compliant man or woman for being contentious.

---

[94] *Hodge's Commentary on Romans, Ephesians and First Corinthians.* See 11:16.

[95] *Gill's Exposition.* (1 Cor.11:16) https://biblehub.com/commentaries/gill/1_corinthians/11.htm

[96] Albert Barnes holds that "it is contrary to custom for women to appear unveiled in public." Mark Dunagan wrote that those who did not adhere to the custom of the day were the contentious or the troublemakers, that as long as veiling was attached to the women's femininity, it was to be observed. Gill, Ellicott and others hold to similar views. Some mention the possibility of 'custom' referring to 'contentiousness', but it is not commentators' preferred interpretation.

[97] *Ellicott's Commentary for English Readers,* (11:16)

[98] *Albert Barnes' Notes on the Whole Bible,* On this passage, Barnes serves as an example of one who assumes that Paul had regulated what man and woman should wear during prayer. The 'contentious' are those who differ with him and all the churches of God.

The Difference Between 'Do' and "Have"

Paul stated, "We <u>have</u> no such custom". (11:16) Moore explains,

> "The evident custom, suggested in the immediate and historical contexts of this passage, is the convention of women covering their heads. Many commentators argue that Paul is here affirming the universal practice of the churches (cf. Buttrick 129; Lowery 159; et al.), but this is just the opposite of what he actually says. He is not appealing to something the churches do, but rather to something the churches do not have. It is not a matter of what was practiced or not practiced in other congregations, but the point is that the head-covering custom was not a Christian dogma. It did not originate with the apostles or the churches. It was not bound by the apostles on the churches. The head-covering was likely worn by Christian ladies in many different regions, but this was part of their culture, not part of their religion. There were things which Paul taught and appointed in every congregation (4.17; 7.17), but this was obviously not one of them. It is wrong to say that human custom is never mentioned in this passage (cf. Jackson 14). Paul makes a distinction between the inspired precepts he had delivered to them (v. 2) and "no such custom" (v. 16)."[99]

"Have" is a verb of possession. It does not say, 'We practice no such custom' or 'we do no such custom.' Lack of a uniform custom was evidence that head covering could not have been one of the 'delivered traditions' Paul had commended them for. (11:2) Therefore, Paul closes his lesson by saying, 'We have no such custom'. If he and the churches 'have' no such custom, then it could not possibly have been a tradition he had delivered and neither could the observance of different customs be reason for his exhortation. (11:2)

Corinth Had a Head Covering 'Doctrine'

The other 'churches of God' had a similar ethnic and religious composite as did the church in Corinth. Different head covering customs of the Romans, Greeks and Jews were not unique to Corinth. But, apparently, the other churches had not adopted a head covering doctrine like the Corinthians had.

---

[99] Kevin L. Moore, *A Critical Analysis of 1 Corinthians 2:11-16*, 1996 P.83

'No Such Practice'   115

"SUCH CUSTOM" WAS NOT HELD AS DOCTRINE

Paul's closing comment is not about what he or the churches did. Paul did not say that he or the churches did not 'do' such a custom. It is about what he and the churches do not have. (hold or possess) Understood in context with his question regarding the propriety of a woman praying with her head uncovered, he is merely saying that he, the other apostles and the churches do not "have" or hold 'such custom' as a doctrine. 'No such custom', would therefore apply to all head covering regulations, not just for women. And, 'no such custom' applies whether the question is answered with 'yes' or 'no'. (11:13,16)

DOES PAUL MEAN A 'CONTENTIOUS' PRACTICE?

On the other hand, if it is deemed that "custom" is a reference to a continual display of contention about head covering, it is also true that he, the other apostles and the churches 'have no such custom'. Fighting for the faith is part of Christian doctrine, but contentions about supposed head covering 'dogma' is not.

Some scholars think 'practice' does not refer to head covering last mentioned in verse 13, but rather to being contentious because it is the nearest antecedent to the phrase, 'no such custom'.[100]

THE DEFINITION OF 'CONTENTIOUS'

The Greek word translated 'contentious' appears nowhere else in the NT. It means 'strife-loving'. Other words translated as 'fight' or 'contend' are used in various contexts to include the believer's right to engage in battle, but head covering was not a matter of contending for the truth. Unequivocally, they were strife-loving, in this case, about head covering.

WHO WERE THE 'STRIFE LOVERS'?

Who were those 'appearing to be contentious? If we know who the contentious party were, we will know the custom Paul had in mind. As mentioned above, the disputatious atmosphere centered on personal opinions about head covering. But, if 'no such custom' pertains to a habit of contention, who were the strife-lovers? As with the other view, it is assumed that the 'practice of contention' pertained to those who did not comply with what was considered the right custom, that they had been the

---

[100] *Lange Commentary on the Holy Scriptures*. This commentary lists commentators who believe that the 'custom' was contentiousness. Henry Alford and others disagree that the 'practice' was a common fault of contentiousness, having discussed head covering in such detail.

ones who were guilty of 'appearing to be contentious'. (11:4,5) But, as stated previously, there is no reason to suppose that the man who prayed with his head covered and the woman who prayed with her head uncovered were contentious. They dishonored no other 'head' but their own! Aa shown previously, this is not the contentious group!

Evidently, those who differed with the non-compliant, engaged in the contentious practice. The woman who prayed covered was not 'dishonored'; the man who prayed uncovered was not dishonored. The two vigorously opposed customs were the man's covered head and the woman's uncovered head during worship. By disapproving alternate customs, they had trampled the rights of others to 'judge in themselves'. This one-sided strife came from those who insisted on one head covering custom for man and the opposite custom for woman.

How Can 'Contentious' Be a Habit?

Most surmise that the 'custom' must be a reference to what the strife was about – head coverings. Is it tenable that 'appearing to be contentious' refer to a habit of strife? Scholars, who disagree with Calvin, argue that one who 'appears contentious' is not a custom.[101] But is this so?

Paul said, 'if anyone appears to be contentious, we have no such custom', which implies a continual pattern of behavior. The verb for 'appears to be' as variously translated. This was a situation where a faction among them were actively appearing contentious. 'Appears to be' is also in the third person, which implies that others could easily discern an active, present, repetitive contentious behavior. This was a current, active 'strife-loving' habit on the part of some in the church, who propagated their head covering view, as exclusive. 'No such practice' comprises the entire idea that this was a present, active contentious campaign of some in the church. Contention could easily be viewed as a habit.

The Two Views Summarized

What then is the custom he or the other apostles or the churches of God did not have? Given everything he had stated to this point, there are only two viable answers to this question: a head covering practice or a contentious practice.

---

[101] *Charles Hodge, Hodge's Commentary on Romans, Ephesians and First Corinthians*, https://www.studylight.org/commentaries/hdg/1-corinthians-11.html

HEAD COVERING PRACTICE

If the favored answer pertains to head covering as mentioned where Paul asks, 'Is it right for a woman to pray uncovered?', then it must be understood that this, or any such practice like it, had not become a doctrine. Neither he, the apostles or the churches were in possession of a creed for the woman's head covering, which also excludes a creed for men.

What does 'no such custom' refer to? According to this interpretation, 'such' is a reference to a specific custom like the woman praying uncovered. This implies three other customs: the woman praying covered, the man praying covered and uncovered. If one is to adopt this view, all four customs are precluded. Whatever one's answer to Paul's question was, he did not have any "such" custom.

CONTENTIOUS PRACTICE

If we side with the scholars who hold that 'custom' refers to a habit of strife, then 'such' contrasts the various customs of head covering with a contentious custom. Strife-loving is sin; wearing a different head covering is not. They had acquired a bad habit of fighting about non-essential, fabricated religious regulations for worship.

On matters pertaining to the salvation and growth, Paul did exhort believers to be prepared to fight as a soldier. (Eph. 6) Jude instructs believers to contend for the faith. (Jude 3) But, as Paul censured any division based on who the speaking minister was, who baptized them, their greed at the Lord's Table, he would also have exhorted them about their strife based on head covering. (3:3-5) Head covering was not a matter of faith and spiritual growth for which believers need to contend. Paul and the churches did not have the practice of judging one another about matters such as head coverings for worship.

WHAT CUSTOMS DID HE HAVE?

Paul's statement, 'We have no such custom' implies that there are other customs he and the churches of God did have. Paul admonished women to dress in a way that professed godliness at all times, not just when believers were assembled together. (1 Tim.2:9,10)

Paul exhorted the churches to ignore efforts to subject one another to religious impositions. He had written to them asking them why they subjected themselves to regulations such as 'do not touch', 'do not taste', 'do not handle'. (Col. 2:20,21) Colossae also had problems with legalism.

Paul mandated and practiced the traditions of the Lord's Table and Baptism. Though not mandated, he practiced Nazarite tradition. But, the customs the Apostles '**have**', are not optional.

Conclusion

Whether 'have no such custom' refers to gender-specific <u>rules for</u> worship head covering, or refers to **strife about** worship head covering, apostolic censure of worship wear did not exist. Either interpretation yields the same conclusion. The Apostles and the churches had no **regulations for** and no **contentions about** head covering.

19 Worship Fashion

Paul had commanded Corinthian believers to judge for themselves what their head covering fashion should be. He, and the other apostles, had no doctrine that demanded head coverings for worship. Erroneous interpretations of 1 Corinthians 11, has fueled a propensity to govern believers' corporate worship and assembly. Paul's advice for the contention swirling around head covering is still relevant for Christians today: 'judge for yourselves'. Not only is head covering an issue. Some believers think that there should be a dress code for church. Similar, to the head covering contention in Corinth, Paul would have advised believers not to let others judge them.

WORSHIP FASHION PRETEXTS

From Paul's exhortation on head covering, helpful principles emerge from this text that can guide our personal demeanor and keep us from needlessly judging others. Following are some <u>faulty</u> pretexts for dressing up or down for church.

ATTIRE SHOWS OTHERS THE IMPORTANCE OF WORSHIP

Some dress up for fellowship and worship because it is their way of showing its special importance in their lives. Such a view is acceptable, if others, who do not share this opinion, are not judged. (11:13) Again, each is to judge for themselves.

How one is dressed does not show what is in his or her heart.

DRESSING UP INCREASES MORALE AND PRODUCTIVITY

Some suggest that morale and productivity are negatively affected by dressing down. Can we 'worship' better if we observe the proper custom? Studies of companies that have allowed casual wear in the office cannot prove this.[102] The morale and productivity of any believer is not determined by clothing. If casual wear does not diminish the believer's spiritual work for the Lord on the other days of the week, neither does his spiritual walk and worship suffer when dressing casual on Sunday.

---

[102] Marisa Sharkey, A study to determine how casual dress in the workplace affects employee morale and productivity, 2000. https://rdw.rowan.edu/cgi/viewcontent.cgi?article=2745&context=etd

FASHION TRADITION SHOWS RESPECT

One of the most curious customs as it pertains to religious expression, is standing, when the Hallelujah Chorus is sung or played. Professing believers might judge the man disrespectful to God for not standing. Do those who remain seated dishonor God? This standing tradition is waning.[103] In one performance a conductor even requested that his audience remain seated during the rendition of the Hallelujah Chorus?[104] But, is that really a bad thing? Does the observance of this tradition really indicate one's relation to the King of Kings? Standing is not necessarily indicative of heartfelt honor for the King of Kings. Not everyone observes this tradition, and often people rise because others do. Looking askance at those who remain seated, is illustrative of how a man with a head covering and a woman without a head covering dishonored their head. Criticisms are based on traditions having no foundation in Scripture. Uniform customs are not required to honor God.

Today, many who attend memorial services do not dress in semi-formal attire, yet intend no disrespect for the family of the deceased. Indeed, an individual known to dress semi-formally for these occasions, shows up at a funeral in jeans and sweat shirt, may be making a negative statement. Usually, a lack of respect, is not reflected by outward appearances.

As the Pharisees, one can be hypocritical whether one is dressed up or dressed down. They would show how they fasted by appearing in public disheveled, with sad and unwashed faces. (Matt. 6:16-18) They enlarged the borders of their robes, wore phylacteries, but Jesus saw them as white-washed sepulchers, full of dead man's bones. (Matt.23:5, 25-28) Like the Corinthians' preoccupation with head coverings; it was all outward showmanship. Traditions do not indicate godliness.

FORMER RELIGIOUS TRADITIONS MUST BE FORSAKEN

Different opinions regarding what should or should not be worn in any public assembly depends on each person's tradition. Even after

---

[103] To Stand or Not To Stand, Most remained seated in a performance of Handel's Messiah in London at Westminster in 2002. It is alleged to have begun when King George II, overwhelmed with the music and its theme stood up during the Hallelujah Chorus portion of Handel's Messiah. Out of respect for the king the entire audience also stood. However, none of this can be proven and King George II never explained why he stood and thus remains a legend. Nobody really knows how this tradition started. http://www.lafolia.com/to-stand-or-not-to-stand/

[104] Tim Page, *'Messiah' a Seasonal Standard Standing Strong*, Washington Post, Dec. 16, 2004, Conductor David Randolph vigorously waved the audience to be seated for the Hallelujah Chorus and Robert Shaw requested that patrons remain seated during HC.

learning that God never required head covering for worship, a woman in Corinth may still have felt more at ease to continue head covering for worship. If her religious sensibilities continued to cause her to feel uncomfortable uncovered during corporate worship, let her cover! But, only then. It is entirely up to her. Conversely, a woman, for whatever reason, may not feel the need to cover her head for worship. In both cases, these women are to be cordially welcomed.

Should a Jewish Christian man wearing a kippah be expected to remove it for worship? According to Paul, he could carry on with his custom at his own discretion. Though Gentiles were not compelled to be circumcised, the Jews still continued with this custom. Former generic religious customs such as head coverings need not be abandoned.

HEAD COVERING INDICATES HEADSHIP

Head covering does not show headship. This had never been a teaching means by which God shows His headship of Christ, Christ's headship of man and man's headship of woman. Head covering does not denote the woman's submission to man; neither does the lack of head covering man's submission to Christ. As discussed at length, headship is depicted by unique autonomous roles, not appearance.

DIFFERENT CUSTOMS HINDERS PEOPLE FROM FELLOWSHIP

Lately, church fashion designers have insinuated that dressing up customs keep people from coming to church. Had Paul thought that it was necessary that everyone should dress the same to bring Jews and Gentiles to worship and fellowship together, he would not have advised the believers to 'judge for themselves'. Interestingly, James did not instruct the rich to dress down; he instructed them to treat the poor the same as he would the rich. (Jas. 2:1-8)

DRESSING UP IS LEGALISTIC

Dressing up as a force of habit from childhood, not expecting others to, is not legalism. According to Paul, continued conformity to one's own custom is not legalism. However, compelling others to conform to a particular obsolete or artificial religious standard is, which was what the Jews were expecting of the Gentiles in Galatia. (Ga.2:14) When someone is guilted into changing a custom based on someone else's opinion, rather than the clear teaching of Scripture, that person has contravened Paul's advice. This is as legalistic as the head covering expectations in Corinth.

Continuing to observe one's own personal preference to wear or not wear a head covering for either man or woman is not legalism. However, judging another's custom for dressing up or down is.

ONE UNIVERSAL CUSTOM IS NECESSARY FOR WITNESS

Some claim that dressing down is a means by which Christians 'become all things to all men in order to save some'. (Rom. 14:14,15; 1 Cor. 9:19-23) By his example, Paul denied himself the liberty to eat meat deemed to be 'unclean', when it might offend the religious sensibilities of recent converts. (1 Cor.8:7) But, in no case did he demand that everyone must stop eating 'unclean' meat.

Head coverings was a completely different issue because adherents to either custom could claim to be 'offended'. The converted Jewish priest and the Roman man could be 'offended' because the Greek did not cover and conversely, the former Greek idolater could be 'offended' because the former Roman idolater and the Jewish priest were still covering. One universal head covering custom was never required for a credible witness.

SUMMARY

The preceding pretexts have all had some negative impact upon believers. Unfortunately, 'worship' is linked to a specific location and day of the week. Jesus taught the disposition of the true worshipper is in spirit and in truth. (Jn. 4:24) In other words, it is possible that people can be dressed up, or down, for 'church', yet fail to worship.

Should the church be in the business of making people look 'acceptable' on the outside? Do we now revert to the religion of the Pharisees who vainly commended themselves to God by their outward appearance? Is this now our witness to the lost who come to hear the gospel at our assembly, that man and woman must comply with specific head covering codes? We know what Paul's answer to these questions would have been: Judge for yourselves.

FASHION PRINCIPLES

Believers are not bound by fashion regulations for worship. However, the Bible does leave us with definite principles for church fashion, customs and trends.

ACCEPTABLE TRADITIONS ARE MODEST

Christian ladies are not to be known by extravagance, either in apparel or hair, but rather by their inward godliness. (1 Pet. 3:3-5) Paul exhorted

Worship Fashion

women not to adorn themselves with costly apparel, whether they are in church or not. (1 Tim.2:9,10) When those who profess godliness wear <u>costly</u> high-end garments and jewelry, they become the focus rather than God. Believers were exhorted not to flaunt their material wealth.

ACCEPTABLE CUSTOMS DO NOT REVEAL THE HEART

Even modestly dressed congregants may have improperly attired hearts, if they have not been clothed with Christ's righteousness. Outward appearance, casual or semi-formal, head covered or not, contributes nothing to acceptable worship.

If God was custom conscious, why did He cause two people die in church for lying to the Holy Spirit? Whether image-conscious Ananias and Sapphira had been dressed up or dressed down, this had no relevance to God's displeasure and their subsequent demise!

ACCEPTABLE CUSTOMS ARE DIVERSE

By exhorting the Corinthians to accept the one another's personal customs, he promoted unity among the brethren. The unity believers have in Christ allows for diverse customs. Uniformity is not the measure of Christian unity.

ACCEPTABLE CUSTOMS ARE APPROPRIATE

Jesus stressed the important of being dressed in the King's righteousness, with a parable of a marriage feast for his son. Someone tried to get in wearing the filthy rags of his own righteousness, rather than accept the wedding garment provided for him. (Matt. 22:11,12) Of course, this was intended to illustrate the necessity of being <u>spiritually</u> dressed appropriately, in the garment of His righteousness. But Jesus' wedding parable implies that the wearing of a wedding garment was not only expected, but also known to be appropriate for weddings.

Imagine. The wedding ceremony has begun. A young man dressed in a tuxedo is standing at the front of the church waiting for his bride to come down the aisle. But, rather than wearing a gorgeous white gown, he sees her dressed in a T-shirt and jeans, flip flopping down the aisle in shower cap. Or, imagine a young bride dressed in a gorgeous white flowing gown, see that the young man standing at the front of the church, who is to be her husband, is wearing a blue t-shirt and orange trousers. That would be a recipe for a much shorter life-span.

I know of no one who had to be told, that dressing for this special occasion was not casual. By nature, people want to be appropriate.

ACCEPTABLE CUSTOMS ARE PERSONAL OPINIONS

'Pastors' have canvassed communities for reasons why they do not come to church. Some alleged that people didn't feel comfortable because church people dress up. Consequently, 'pastors' promoted 'dressing down' as part of a seeker-sensitive program to increase attendance.

Rather than demanding people comply with a single head covering custom, Paul left it entirely up to every individual. He was sensitive to the seekers' <u>need</u> for the gospel, not their desire to <u>feel comfortable</u> in the 'holy' attire of a favored head covering custom. He made people feel uncomfortable for breaking God's Law, not for 'violating' an unfamiliar head covering tradition.

ACCEPTABLE CUSTOMS MUST NOT DISHONOR CHRIST

While the Bible allows considerable latitude, it becomes obvious that some customs are rituals inherited from a former religion. For example, in praying the rosary, both Mary and the Father are prayed to. This, of course, is blasphemous and would not be permitted in the fellowship. On the other hand, some 'Christians' believe that baptism is our ticket to heaven. Despite this false teaching, believers still practice baptism, to show that by repentance and faith, not baptism, the Spirit has washed their sin away.

SUMMARY

In our fellowship with believers, we should dress in a way that does not distract from the apparel of the righteousness God has given to each of His children. Women and men are to be guided by their conscience as it is informed by Scripture and nature. Compelling conformity compromises our right to judge for ourselves. As children of God, our job is not to please others by what we wear. Knowing that God sees our heart, we ought to be very slow to judge another's motives by their outward appearance. Different customs are not the measure of the believer's walk with the Lord.

20 Judging Others

The church in Corinth was judging others. They dishonored others, whose preferred worship custom differed with theirs, further fueling their divisions and distracting the church from her gospel mission of salvation and sanctification. It was a judgmental church.

In a similar vein, Paul also cites other churches for judging others.

PAUL INCRIMINATED OTHER CHURCHES

Judging others was also a problem among the churches of Galatia, Colossae and Rome. Fellowship among Jews and Gentiles was jeopardized by requiring traditions in other churches, as well as Corinth.

THE ASSEMBLIES IN GALATIA

A division had also developed in the churches of Galatia between Jews and Gentiles based on custom. Jews were pressuring Gentiles to live like Jews. Peter, having previously eaten with the Gentiles, ate only with the Jews and Paul exhorted him publicly for it. False Jewish believers were teaching that Mosaic traditions, such as circumcision, were a means of salvation through Christ. Deeply troubled, Paul asked them, "Who has bewitched you...?" (Ga. 3:1) If they could not justify themselves by means of the works of the Moral Law, how could they justify themselves with ceremonial law? Human effort to do the works of the law, moral or ceremonial, could neither save or sanctify. Yet, even Peter allowed himself to be judged on the externals of religious customs. (Ga. 2:1-16)

THE ASSEMBLY IN COLOSSAE

Paul also addressed a similar situation in Colossae. Certain foods and holy days, no doubt based in Judaism, had become a means of judging one another. Apparently, some professing believers had been puffing themselves up by subjecting themselves to temporal Jewish ordinances, that had never provided spiritual sustenance or growth. Like the Corinthians, their quest for spirituality was based on fleshly doctrines of men, 'touch not; taste not; handle not', and therefore futile.

Paul's answer is provided at the beginning of his summary of the problem, "Let no man judge you...". This implies, of course, that each person is to judge for himself, just as he instructed the Corinthians on head covering. Outward religious customs were not forbidden, neither were they required. (Col. 2:16-23) They, too, were judgmental of others.

THE ASSEMBLY IN ROME

Believers in Rome had apparently also been passing judgment upon one another due to different customs of Jews and Gentiles. Unaware of the meaning of their rites and ceremonies, the Jews boasted in their outward display and performance of religion. (Rom. 2:24-29; 3:27-31; 4:5-12) Impacted by a history of Mosaic and contrived traditions, the Jews not only wanted to keep them, but also require them of Gentile believers. Gentiles were judged inferior because they were uncircumcised. Paul explained that without spiritual circumcision, this tradition meant nothing. The Jewish 'advantage' was of no avail, if their heart remained uncircumcised. (Rom. 2:28, 29; 3:1)

The Jews judged Gentile believers based on the outward keeping of ceremonial law. So, Paul ruled that diverse customs regarding Sabbaths and diet were to be permitted among Jews and Gentiles. Each one must be persuaded in his own mind. (Rom. 14:1-6)

SUMMARY

The Jews judged and even tried to compel others to perform external religious laws. Paul's theme is the same: do not judge others or allow yourself to be judged by others.

SUMMARY OF THE APOSTLE'S RULINGS

Paul's tactic against the imposition of religious customs in the other churches was similar to his advice on head coverings.

BE PERSUADED BY YOUR OWN MIND.

Paul counsels the church to receive the weak in the faith with one caveat. Given the propensity of Jews, especially, to argue for tradition, the Apostle precludes the disputatious. (Rom. 14:1) Weak believers were to be received, but the church was to be wary of any legalistic ploys. Anyone, whose purpose it was to make diet and Sabbaths mandatory, should not be received.

Jesus helps us to know who the weaker brother is not. Jesus purposely offended the Jewish elites who observed the laws of the Sabbath. (Matt. 12) His disciples did not wash their hands as prescribed in the OT. (Matt.

Judging Others

15:2) These Jews were Christ' antagonists, disputing optional matters. They were not His brothers.

Each person is to be persuaded according to his own mind, not someone else's. (Rom. 14:1-6)

DO NOT JUDGE YOUR BROTHER

Yet, being persuaded in one's own mind about religious customs, is not a license to judge others who have an entirely different opinion. Therefore, different views about traditions are not a sufficient reason to judge. Christ is our Judge, not our brother. (Rom. 14:10)

'DO NOT JUDGE ONE ANOTHER'

Though Paul was convinced by the Lord that there was nothing inherently unclean, yet, new believers among them, still thought eating meat offered to idols was. Rather than 'judging' them to be wrong, he advised more mature believers to judge whether a new believer had been offended. Instead of judging one another; judge the issues common to new Jew and Gentile believers that might be stumbling blocks to spiritual growth. (Rom. 14:13-15)

'JUDGE FOR YOURSELVES'

Naturally, the pagan Greek man who did not cover and the pagan Roman who covered, when worshipping idols, would be inclined to continue with their respective customs after conversion. If the Greek, who had always worshiped his gods with head uncovered, why should he, as a new believer, be required to cover and conversely, if a Roman, who had always worshiped the gods, covered, be expected to uncover? Paul's ruling to the Corinthian church was, 'judge for yourselves'.

SUMMARY

Religious customs passed down through the Mosaic Law were no longer compulsory. The prophetic imagery of the Mosaic ceremonies and rituals had been fulfilled by Christ's death and resurrection. Jew and Gentile believers could now fellowship together without outward religious customs.

In the likelihood that new Jewish converts continue to abhor eating 'unclean' meat, and new Gentile believers now despise eating meat that had been sacrificed to idols they had worshiped, Paul exhorted mature believers to abstain from eating this meat, for the sake of the conscience of the weaker brother. (Rom. 14:13-19; 1 Cor. 8:7-13) Neither eating meat sacrificed to idols could make one better or worse, but it could distract some from fellowship with one another and with God. So, if, for this reason, a new believer was grieved, Paul advised mature believers to indulge the weaker brother by abstaining from this otherwise legitimate food. However, even eating meat offered to idols was permitted, except when new believers might be hindered in their walk with the Lord.[105]

Even from this brief review of Paul's letters to other churches, it is apparent Corinth was not unique to judgmentalism. Without any OT basis, worship head covering had become yet another external metric by which believers could judge one another. To all the churches, Paul's message was consistent. He commanded believers to be 'persuaded in their own mind', 'not to judge others' and to 'judge for yourselves'. He had also decreed that believers not permit anyone to pass judgment on others, regarding religious customs. (Col. 2:16,17) Traditions are optional.

Paul wanted unity of the spirit, not uniformity of the flesh.

JAMES' EXHORTATION

James addressed a similar problem. Professing Jewish believers were showing special favor to those who wore expensive clothing and jewelry. He exhorted them not to base their respect for others on their outward appearance and possessions. (Jas. 2:2-4) They were thinking 'evil' of the poorly dressed, without cause. They were judging others.

WHO CANNOT JUDGE HEAD COVERING?

The Corinthian head covering conflict bears no resemblance to the grief of a new believer, who saw his Jewish or Gentile brother eat meat offered to idols. Reasons for the offense of eating 'unclean' meat were common to Jew and Gentile; head covering protocol was not.

Different head covering customs of Jewish, Greek and Roman unbelievers must all be accepted. Jewish priests and Romans would see that the Greek custom was favored. What would a Roman man think about Greek men who worshiped with their head uncovered? Who should determine worship head covering protocol? Paul's answer is, 'neither'. No person, Jew or Gentile, is allowed to judge another's head covering.

---

[105] Since spiritual growth is expected from new sensitive weak believers, stumbling blocks must have an expiry date.

Judging Others

To overlook the actual grammar and imperatives of the biblical texts, is to cover the truth with religious haze, such that Paul's exhortation on the head covering custom is blurred beyond recognition. Thus, ecclesial authorities have presumed a biblical imperative for worship, where there is none. Ecclesial authorities cannot judge head covering.

The presence or absence of head covering for worship, was strictly a personal matter, not subject to the judgment of others.

The Final Judgment

Left to man's fleshly, religious sentiments, he would continue to invent and impose customs for worship, just like the Pharisees did. Worship wear cannot distract God from looking into our heart. (Heb. 4:13) He looks into the heart of the worshipper, to see if man or woman has truly repented of sin and turned by faith to Christ alone for salvation. Only then, in the righteousness that Christ Himself provides, is he or she clothed acceptably for worship.

Paul echoes his exhortation to the Corinthians, when he addressed the outward religion of the Colossians, 'let no man judge you'. No head covering tradition eliminates conflict and no head covering tradition qualifies one to worship God.

We are not to judge others.

It is no surprise, then, that Paul's judgment on the matter is, **'Judge in you yourselves.'**

ABOUT THE AUTHOR

Raised by Christian parents in conservative churches, Bible teaching has greatly benefited Howard Boldt from childhood. Since Bible College, he served in church administration, music, and teaching Sunday and mid-week Bible classes. With his growing interest in the Scriptures, Howard became particularly concerned about the negative impact doctrinal errors were having upon Christians. From teaching to essays to books, he has attempted to articulate biblical reasoning for his views. Happily married to his wife of 51 years, he has also experienced the joys of family life. He lives in Alberta, Canada.

www.ingramcontent.com/pod-product-compliance
Lightning Source LLC
LaVergne TN
LVHW051605070426
835507LV00021B/2783